Ignacio Larrañaga

ENCOUNTER

Prayer Handbook

New Revised Edition

MÉDIASPAUL

Canadian Cataloguing in Publication Data

Larrañaga, Ignacio

Encounter: prayer handbook

Translation of: Encuentro

ISBN 2-89420-125-7

1. Catholic Church – Prayer books and devotions –
English. I. Title.

BX2130.L37 1998   242'.802   C98-940396-3

Originally published as *Encuentro*,
Ediciones Cefepal, Santiago, Chile, 1989.

Phototypesetting: *Médiaspaul*

Cover: *Mike Lory - Summum*

ISBN 2-89420-125-7

Legal Deposit – 3rd Quarter 1998
Bibliothèque nationale du Québec
National Library of Canada

© 1998 Éditions Médiaspaul
             250, boul. Saint-François Nord
             Sherbrooke, QC, J1E 2B9 (Canada)

CONTENTS

To Pray

FOREWORD

(To the 7th Spanish Edition)

For many years, I have used the book Hymns and Prayers for the Encounters—An Experience with God. *In it were texts gleaned from many sources and added to my own, texts appropriate to the tone of the Encounters.*

For this book, I have developed a series of poems and songs appropriate for different states of mind, and diverse life situations.

I have included several elements from the previous book, although I have eliminated a substantial part of its contents. Since the authors of some of these compositions are unknown, I preferred not to mention any names.

I have included many Bible quotations, methods of prayer, various exercises, and practical orienta-

tions; everything abridged and simplified to its utmost. I strove to place in the hands of the reader a few simple and effective guidelines—as a Manual to help you in the art of praying.

Those prayers written by me are the following: 1, 2, 10, 13, 15, 17, 19, 20, 21, 22, 23, 24, 25, 26, 28, 34, 36, 37, 41, 43, 45, 47, 48, 51, 53, 55, 58, 59, 60. Others belong to different authors, and some have been modified.

This edition is final and will not be altered in the future.

Ignacio Larrañaga

PRAYERS

I. THE LORD

1. *Center of Gravity*

To sing of you, Lord Jesus, how I wish my
eyes were those of an eagle, my heart that of a
child and my tongue that of a poet, my whole
being burnished by silence!

Touch my heart, Lord Jesus Christ, touch it
and the dreams concealed in the human roots
since the beginning of the world will awaken.

All our voices come together at your doors.
All our waves vanish on your beaches.
All our winds sleep on your horizon.
Without knowing it, our most secret desires
long after you and implore you.
The profoundest yearnings
look impatiently for you.
You are a starry night,
a glowing music,
the vortex of the universe, a fire from flint.

Where you place your wounded foot
the planet is ablaze in blood and gold.

You walk on singing waters
and over snowy tops,
you whisper in age-old forests.
You smile in the myrtle.
You breathe in algae,
mushrooms and lichen.
I sense you are being born,
growing, living, laughing, talking
in the whole mineral and vegetable world.

You are the pulse of the world, my Lord
Jesus Christ. You are the One who unceasingly
comes from far away galaxies,
from the burning center of the earth,
and from the night of time;
your origin is forever,
from millions of light-years away.

On your brow shines the destiny
of the world, and in your heart
is concentrated the fire of centuries.

My heart is dazzled by so many wonders,
and bowing down, I say:
You will be the King of my dominions.

For you are the fire of my blood.
You shall be my path and my light,
the cause of my joy,

the reason of my existence
and the purpose of my life,
my compass and horizon,
my ideal, my wholeness
and my fulfillment.
Outside of you there is nothing for me.

My last song shall be yours.
Glory and honor are yours forever,
King of all ages!

2. *Father*

How shall I call you,
you who has no name?

Your son Jesus
came forth from the depths
of your solitude.
He told us that you existed
and that your name was *Father*.
This was great news.

In the quiet afternoon of eternity,
when you were life and expanding fire,
I lived in your mind.
You cherished me like a golden dream,

and my name was written
on the palm of your right hand.
I did not deserve this,
but you loved me without a reason.
You loved me as one does his only child.

From the night of my solitude
I lift my arms to tell you: oh Love,
most holy Father, tireless sea of tenderness,
cover me with your presence,
for I am cold
and sometimes everything frightens me.
It is said that where there is love
there is no fear.
Why then do these dark currents
drag me towards unknown worlds
of anxiety, fear, and apprehension?
Beloved Father, have mercy
and grant me the gift of peace,
the peace found on a sunset.

I know you are the loving presence,
surrounding love,
infinite woodland of protection.

You are pardon and understanding,
security and certainty, joy and freedom.

I go out on the street and you are with me;
I get engrossed in work
and you remain at my side;
in agony and beyond
you say to me: here I am, I go with you.

Even if I try to escape your circle of love,
climb mountains or stars,
even if I were able to fly away
all is useless.

I cannot avoid your chase.
You circle me, engulf me
and transfigure me.

I was told your feet walked
across worlds and centuries
in search of my fleeing shadow,
and that when you found me
the sky broke open with songs.
With all this good news
you have transformed me
into a prodigiously free child.
Thank you.

Now make my old castles and the high walls
of my selfishness crumble until there is nothing

left of me, not even my dust,
and thus I may be transparent for my brothers.

Then while I go through
desolate worlds,
I will also be tenderness and refuge.
I will enlighten the night of pilgrims,
I will tell orphans: "I am your mother."
I will give shade to the exhausted,
a native land to fugitives,
and the ones who lack a home
will find shelter under my roof.

You are my home and my native land.
I wish to rest in this home
at the end of the battle.

You will certainly watch over my sleep,
Father, eternally loving and loved.
Amen.

3. *Illuminating Light*

Once more, Lord,
we live a profound intimacy.
Each one of us feels his life
marvelously invaded by your life.

We are now living the adventure
of your life in our life,
your strength in our weakness,
your vigor in our helplessness.
Your light has entered
the paths of my being.
You are light for my path.
I know that only in your light, Lord,
will I be able to build my life beautifully.

I know you live in the light,
and that you have passed on
some of this light to us.

But, unfortunately,
all is darkness on our part.

Lord, people seem content
to walk in the dark.
They seem content
walking as blind persons,
with a bandage over their eyes.
They do not want to see.
This is also my sin;
very often I do not want to see.

I fear that if I look at my life
I will have to change.
I implore you, Lord: open my eyes.

In this instant of honesty, I am sure, Lord,
I am certain I want to see.
Let your light
penetrate my darkness, now.
Light, clarity, brightness, blinding light.
Transparent clearness, illuminating flash.

I want to see, Lord, I want to see. Amen.

4. *You Came As a Friend*

You came and offered me
your friendship,
humbly and discreetly.
You lifted me to your level,
coming down to mine,
and you wish for an intimate relationship,
full of mutual surrender.

You mysteriously remain in me,
as an ever-present friend;
you always give yourself to me,
and fulfil all my aspirations
completely.

When you give yourself to us,
with you, we possess all of creation,

since the whole universe belongs to you.
So that our friendship would be a perfect one,
you made me an associate
to your sufferings and joys;
you shared with me your hopes,
your projects, your life.

You invite me to share
in your work of redemption,
to put all my strength to work with you.

You want our friendship
to be a fruitful and productive one
for myself and for others.

God, friend of man and woman,
Creator, friend of all creatures,
Holy one, friend of the sinner.

You are the ideal friend,
one that never fails
and never says no.

I would like to respond to
the offering of such a magnificent friendship,
in the way that you hope
and deserve that I do,
always acting as your friend. Amen.

5. I Gave You So Little

I gave you so little, Lord Jesus,
but you turned it into something grand!
I am so small before you,
and you make me so rich!

I did not give all that
I had wished, nor did
I love you as I had wished and dreamt.

I gave you so little, truly so little,
and with such little enthusiasm and joy.

Nonetheless, you know that I wanted
to dedicate my heart in that "little".

You see the depths of my being,
my desire to give you so much more.

Since you transform my poverty into riches,
and my emptiness into fullness,
take my gift just as it is.
Take also what it is not,
so that my surrender will be total
even with my own misery,
and once more all will be recreated
by the supreme power of your love. Amen.

6. We Need You

We need you, only you, and nothing more than you. You, who loves us, only you can feel all we suffer, the compassion each of us feels for himself. Only you can measure how great a need the world has of you, at this time.

Everyone needs you, even those who do not know it; they need you much more than those who know.

The hungry think they must seek bread, while they hunger for you; the thirsty think they need water, when they thirst for you. The sick have unfounded hopes to find health; their real misfortune is your absence. Those who seek the beauty of the world, without knowing it seek you, the fullness of beauty. Those who look for the truth in their thoughts, without knowing it, long for you, the only truth worth knowing. Those who seek peace look for you, the only peace anxious hearts can find.

They call you without knowing it, and their cry is more distressing than ours. We need you. Come, Lord.

7. I Seek Your Face, Lord

Leave your daily worries for a moment, insignificant one; enter for an instant within yourself; withdraw from your confused thoughts and the worries which oppress you. Rest in God for only and instant.

Enter into the depth of your soul. Withdraw from everything except God and whatever can help you to find him. Close the door of your room and look for him in silence.

Tell God with all your might, tell the Lord: I seek your face. Your face I seek, Lord.

And now, my Lord and my God, show me how and where I have to look for you, where and how I can find you.

If you are not in me, Lord, if you are absent, where will I find you? If you are everywhere, why don't you make yourself present? It is true that you live in an inaccessible light, but where is that inaccessible light? How will I reach it? Who will guide me into the light so that I may contemplate you there? In what signs will I recognize you? I have never seen you, my Lord and my God. I do not know your face.

God most high, what will this forsaken one do without you? What will this servant do, thirsting for your love, roaming far from you? I want to see you but your face is far away from me. I want to be close to you but your dwelling place is inaccessible. I burn with the desire to find you but I ignore where you dwell. I sigh for you but have never seen your face.

Lord, you are my God. You are my Lord, but I do not know you. You made me and you redeemed me. You asked for all I have, but still I do not know you. I was made to see you, and yet I have not reached the end for which I was created.

And you Lord, how long will you forget us? How long will you hide your face?

When will you look toward us? When will you listen to us? When will you open your eyes and show us your face? When will you answer our desires?

Lord, hear us, enlighten us, reveal yourself to us. Heed our needs, and we will be happy.

Without you all is annoying and sad. Have mercy on us in our work and in the efforts we make to reach you, for without you we can do nothing.

Show me how to seek you. Show me your face, for if you do not, I will not find you. I will not be able to find you unless you make yourself present. I will seek you as I desire you. I will desire you as I seek you. Loving you I will find you, and finding you I will love you. Amen.

8. *Adoration*

Oh my God, trinity whom I adore, help me forget myself so that I may be rooted in you, motionless and calm as though my soul were already in eternity. May nothing be able to disturb my peace nor separate me from you, my immutable God, but may every moment carry me further into the depths of your mystery.

Calm my soul. Make it your heaven, your cherished abode, and the place of your rest; may I never abandon you; in attentive faith may I remain immersed in you, in a state of adoration, in total surrender to your creative action.

Oh my beloved Christ, crucified by love, may I be a soulmate after your own heart; may I cover you with glory and love you unto death! I realize my weakness and beg you to clothe me with yourself, identify my soul with all the movements of your heart; I beg you to embrace me, to lift me, immerse within me, substitute yourself for me, so that my life may be but a radiance of your own. Come and dwell in me as adorer, as restorer, and as savior.

Oh eternal Word, expression of my God, may I spend my life listening to you; may I become completely docile so that I may learn everything from you; then, through all the nights and emptiness, in all my times of helplessness, may I ever cling to you and dwell in your great light. Oh my beloved star, enchant me so that I can never turn from your radiance.

Oh consuming fire, spirit of love, descend upon me so that in my soul there may be a new incarnation of the word, so that I may be to

Him a new humanity wherein He renews all his mystery.

And you, Oh Father, incline yourself toward this poor creature, and overshadow me, seeing in me only your beloved Son in whom you are well pleased.

Oh my "Three", my all, my beatitude, infinite solitude, immensity wherein I lose myself, I surrender myself to you as your prey. Immerse yourself in me so that I may be immersed in you, with the hope that I will contemplate the depths of your greatness in your light. Amen.

9. Invocation of the Holy Spirit

Holy Spirit, Lord of light,
from your clear celestial height,
your pure beaming radiance give.
Come, Oh Father of the poor,
come with treasures that endure,
come, Oh Light of all that lives.
You of all consolers best,
and the soul's delightsome guest,
do refreshing peace bestow.
You in toil are comfort sweet,

pleasant coolness in the heat,
solace in the midst of woe.

Light immortal, light divine,
visit now this heart of mine,
and my inmost being fill.
If you take your grace away;
nothing pure in us will stay,
all our good is turned to ill.

Heal our wounds, our strength renew,
on our dryness pour your dew,
wash the stains of guilt away.
Bend the stubborn heart and will,
melt the frozen, warm the chill,
guide the steps that go astray.

On all those who evermore
you confess and you adore,
in your sevenfold gifts descend.
Give them comfort when they die.
Give them life with you on high,
give them joys that never end.

II. FAITH, HOPE

10. Consolation

Lord, Lord. I can't go on anymore.
I have spent a long night
immersed in salty waters. Be merciful.
Loneliness is a high wall
that shuts all horizons.
I lift up my eyes but I see nothing.

My family turned their back on me
and left.
All of them left.
Desolation is my company;
anguish is my food.
There are no roses left, everything is sadness.
Where are you, my Father?
A cruel agony is frozen and trapped
in the deepest part of me.

Give me your hand, Father, hold me;
take me out of this dark prison.
Don't close the door, please, for I am alone.
Why do you remain silent?

My screams fill the night,
but you remain deaf and mute.

Wake up, my Father.
Give me at least one signal that you live,
that you love me, that you are here,
now, with me.
The frightening darkness surrounds me,
it scares me,
and I have only you
as my defense.

But I know the morning will return,
and you will comfort me again
as a mother comforts her child;
and harmony will cover the horizon,
and rivers of consolation
will flow through my veins.

My family will return to my presence,
and there will be new shoots and stars,
and the air will be filled with joy,
and the night with song,
and my soul will sing
your mercy eternally,
because you have consoled me.
Thank you, my Father. Amen.

11. *Those Who Believe*

Blessed are those who did not see you,
yet believed in you.

Blessed are those who did not
contemplate your image
and proclaimed your divinity.
Blessed are those who, in reading the Gospel,
have recognized in you the very One
they hoped for.
Blessed are those who, in your envoys,
discerned your divine presence.

Blessed are those who,
in their innermost heart,
heard your voice and responded.
Blessed are those who,
encouraged by the desire to touch God,
have found you in the silence.
Blessed are those who,
in times of darkness,
clung more strongly to your light.

Blessed are those who,
in the hour of darkness,
maintain their confidence in you.
Blessed are those who,

perceiving your absence,
go on believing in your closeness.
Blessed are those who, not having seen you,
live in the secure hope
of seeing you one day. Amen.

12. *Moments of Obscurity*

Lord Jesus Christ,
out of the darkness of death
you brought forth the light.
In the deep and profoundest solitude lives,
from now and forever,
the powerful protection of your love.
From the deep we can now sing
the alleluia of those who are saved.

Grant us the humble simplicity of faith,
one that does not vanish when you hound us
in hours of obscurity and abandonment,
when everything becomes problematic.

In these times
when a mortal battle surrounds us,
grant us enough light
not to lose sight of you,
enough light

to those who need it
more than we do.

Make the mystery of your paschal joy
shine upon us like the dawn.
Allow us to become
real paschal people in the midst
of this holy Saturday of history.

Grant us that, across the bright
or gloomy days of our times,
we may always walk with joyfulness
towards the glory to come. Amen.

13. *Hidden Presence*

You are not there.
We cannot see your face.
You are there.
Your rays burst in all directions.
You are the Hidden Presence.

Oh! Presence always hidden
and always clear,
Oh! fascinating mystery
towards which
every aspiration focuses.

Oh! intoxicating wine
that satisfies all desires.
Oh! unfathomable infinite
that soothes all delusions.

You are the furthest and closest of all.
Your substance dwells
in my entire being.
You bestow existence
and consistency upon me.

You penetrate me,
you surround me, you love me.

You are around me and in me.
With your active presence you reach
the remotest and deepest zones
of my intimacy.

You are the soul of my soul,
the life of my life,
more me than myself,
total and totalizing reality,
in the midst of which I am submerged.
With your vivifying force
you penetrate all that I am, all that I have.

Take me entirely,
all of my all,

and make me
a living transparency
of your being and of your love,
Oh! most beloved Father.

14. Lord of Victory

When all our human projects,
our earthly supports disintegrate,
when out of our most beautiful dreams
only disillusionment is left,
when our best efforts
and our firmest desires
do not reach the proposed objective,
when sincerity and loving zeal
obtain nothing,
and failure is present, distressing and cruel,
frustrating our most beautiful hopes,
Lord, you remain indestructible and strong,
a friend who can do everything.

Your plans remain unchanged,
nothing can stop your will
to be fulfilled.
Your dreams are more beautiful than ours,
and you make them come true.

You transform failure into triumph;
you are never defeated.
You, who from emptiness
create all beings and all life,
take our powerlessness
into your creative hands,
with infinite love,
and make it produce the fruit of your work,
beyond all our desires.
In you, our hope
is saved from disaster
and realized. Thank you. Amen.

15. *God of Faith*

Oh! You who have no name
and are intangible like a shadow
but solid as a rock!
You will never be captured
through our efforts
nor mastered through intellectual activity,
for you are the God of faith.

You are not something mysterious
but mystery;

One who cannot be
understood analytically;
One who will not be reduced
to abstractions nor categories.
One who will never be reached
by syllogisms;
One who is to be received,
taken on, lived.
One who is "understood"
surrendering ourselves
on our knees in faith.
Your are the God of faith.

The most excellent words of the human
language will never be able to confine the
slightest bit of your substance. They will not
be able to embrace the fullness, the immensity
and the depth of your reality.

You surpass, contain, reach and comprise
all names and all words.
You are the One-Without-Name,
truly the Unnamed.
You are the God of faith.

Only in the profound night of faith,
when the mind is quiet,

in total silence, and in the total presence,
knees bent and heart open,
only then does the certainty of faith appear.
Night turns into day, and one begins
to understand the unintelligible.

All the while, we faintly discern your face
between semi-darkness, signs, vestiges,
analogies, and comparisons.
But face to face, one cannot see you.
You are the God of faith.

Our ardent desire is to hold on to you,
to adhere to you.
We wish to possess you,
to adjust to you, and to rest in you.
But how often,
when we come close to your threshold,
you vanish like a dream, and once more
become absence and silence.

You are definitely the God of faith.

Like exiles, we are pulled toward you by an
obscure and powerful nostalgia, a strange
nostalgia for a person we have never embraced
and a native land we have never inhabited.

You give us the appetizer and leave us without the banquet. You give us the first fruits, but not the delight of the kingdom. You give us your shadow, but not your face, and you leave us like a taut bow. Where are you?

Pilgrims of the absolute and seekers of an infinite, we shall never find you, and since we will never "meet" you, we are destined to always walk behind you like eternal pilgrims on an odyssey that will not end until we reach the ultimate shores of the homeland, when faith and hope are no longer necessary, and only love remains. Then, yes, we shall contemplate you face to face.

My God, if I am an echo of your voice, how is it that the echo continues to vibrate while the voice remains silent?

If I am thirsty, and you are immortal water, when will this thirst be quenched?

If I am the river, and you the sea,
when will I rest in you?
I acclaim you and proclaim you,
I affirm you and confirm you,
I call for you and need you,

41

I yearn for you and long for you,
where are you?

Before you, who have neither name nor face,
in the darkness of the night,
I fall on my knees,
I surrender to you, I believe in you.

16. *Prayer of Hope*

Lord,
I am once again before your mystery.
I am constantly embraced by your presence
that is so often transformed into absence.
I look for your presence
in the absence of your presence.

When I look at the immensity of the world
I am under the impression
that many no longer have hope in you.
Even I make my own plans, set my goals,
and lay the stones of a building
that seems to have
no other architect but me.

Nowadays,
we are often creatures

who set our hopes in ourselves.
Give me, Lord,
the most profound conviction
that I will destroy my future
if hope in you
is not present.

Make me understand deeply that,
in spite of the chaos of things around me,
in spite of the nights that I must overcome,
in spite of the weariness of my days,
my future is in your hands.
Make me see
that the earth you show me
on the horizon of the day to come
will be more beautiful and better.

I lay my steps and my days
into your mystery,
for I know that your Son,
my brother,
has conquered despair
and guaranteed me a new future
because he has risen from death to life.
Amen.

17. Suffering and Redemption

Lord, what is the meaning of being a man, a woman? To endure pain and suffering. From the cries of the newborn to the last groan of the dying, suffering is the daily and bitter bread that never lacks on the family table.

My God, what good is suffering? It is a useless waste. It has no name, but it does have a thousand sources and a thousand faces, and who can avoid it? It walks by our side on the road that leads from darkness to light. What can be done with it?

It is a creature that grew out of the human soil like a cursed fungus, without being planted or wanted. What can we do with it?

I remember your cross. Oh humble Jesus of Nazareth; you did not choose this cross, but accepted it not joyfully but peacefully. Of what use is this vast current of human suffering? That is the question: what can be done with this essential and burning mystery?

Thousands of illnesses, a thousand and one misunderstandings, intimate conflicts, nervous breakdowns and obsessions, resentments and envies, melancholies and sadness, limitations and helplessness, our own and that of others, pains, nails, tortures. Of what use can this endless forest of dead leaves be?

You, the just one, the obedient and submissive servant of the Father, when your hour came, (after you quivered with fear), you surrendered yourself peacefully, and you freely accepted to drain the cup of sorrow to its bitter end. Actions of human conspiracy did not fall upon you blind and fatal, but you took them on voluntarily, knowing that they were not due to human intrigue, that the Father permitted them. You carried your cross with love.

I thank you for the lesson, Christ, my friend. We now have the answer to the fundamental question of man: what can be done with suffering?

Suffering is not conquered by complaining, by fighting or by resisting, but by taking it on. When we take on our cross lovingly, not only do we accompany you, Jesus of Nazareth, on the road to Calvary, but we cooperate with you in the redemption of the world. And much more, "we make up for what is lacking to the passion of the Lord."

Perfect freedom consists not only of taking up the cross with love, but to be grateful for it, to know that in this manner we take on human suffering and we participate in the transcendent task of redeeming humanity.

I thank you, Lord Jesus Christ, for the wisdom of the cross.

III. CIRCUMSTANCES

18. Morning Prayer

Lord, in the silence of this new day,
I open the door to peace.
I come to ask you for peace,
wisdom and strength.
Today, I want to look at the world
with eyes filled with love;
I want to be patient,
understanding, humble, meek, and good.
To see your children beyond
their outward appearance,
as you see them yourself,
in order to appreciate
the kindness of each one.
Close my ears to idle words,
keep my tongue from gossip,
that I may only have
thoughts of blessing.
I want to be so well-intentioned and just
that all who approach me
may feel your presence.

Clothe me, Lord, with your goodness,
and may I be a reflection of you
throughout this day. Amen.

19. *Evening Prayer*

My father, now that voices have hushed
and the cries have ceased,
my soul rises to you to say:
I believe in you, I have hope in you,
I love you with all my might.
Glory to you, Lord.

I surrender into your hands the fatigue and
the battles, the joys and disappointments
of this day which has ended.

If my nerves betrayed me, if self-centered
impulses had the best of me, If I allowed
resentment or melancholy to invade me,
forgive me, Lord. Have mercy on me.

If I was unfaithful, if my mouth spoke
idle words, if I let myself be overcome
by impatience, if I was a thorn for someone,
forgive me, Lord. I do not want to fall asleep
without feeling in my soul the safety
of your sweet and unbinding mercy.

I give you thanks, my Father, for you were the refreshing shadow that shielded me all through the day. I give you thanks because all through these hours you surrounded me—invisible, affectionate—you watched over me like a mother.

Lord, around me all is silent and calm. Send the angel of peace over this house. Relax my nerves, appease my spirit, set my mind at rest, flood my being with silence and serenity.

Watch over me, beloved Father,
when I surrender myself to sleep,
as confident as a child
who sleeps happily in your arms.
In your name, Lord, I will rest peacefully.
Amen.

20. In Times of Sickness

I pray for health to you, Lord, who passed through this world healing all sickness and pain. I cry out as a poor tree scourged by pain. Son of David, have mercy on me.

My health is failing like a crumbling sand castle. I am enclosed in a fatal circle; the hospital, the bed, the tests, the diagnosis, the alcohol, the cotton, the nurse; I cannot leave that circle. I feel a beast in the innermost part of my body but no one finds it. Have mercy on me, Lord.

My God, every morning I wake up tired. My eyes are red from sleeplessness. I often feel as heavy as a bag of sand. My bones feel like they have been eaten away, my insides feel torn. Pain gnaws me like a mad dog, and above all I fear, Lord.

I am very frightened. Fear clings to my soul like a wet garment. What will become of me? Will the dawn of health come upon me? Will I be able to sing the glory of the healed someday?

My God, when will you visit me? Didn't you say: "Arise and walk?" Didn't you say to Lazarus, "Come out?" Didn't the lepers heal and the lame walk at the command of your voice? Didn't you order: "Let go of your crutches", "Walk on water?" When will my hour come? When may I also sing your wonders? Son of David, have mercy on me. You are my only hope.

And yet I know there is something worse than sickness: anxiety. Health is good but peace is still better. What good is health without peace? And what I need, most of all, is peace, my Lord Jesus Christ. Anxiety, loneliness, fear, uncertainty, and anguish assault me and at times totally dominate me. Frequently, I feel sadness, and at times, deadly sadness.

I need peace, Lord Jesus, that peace that you alone can give. Give me that peace which is consolation, that peace which is the fruit of total surrender. Therefore, I place my health in the hands of physicians and will do all that is possible to regain it. The rest I leave in your hands.

From this very moment, I let go of the oars and allow my boat to drift in your divine currents.

Lead me wherever you wish, Lord. Give me health and long life. May it be done according to your will and not my desire. I know tonight you will console me. Fill me with your serenity. That is all I ask. Amen.

51

21. Marriage Garland

Lord, one day on the bare ground
there suddenly a flower
of snow and fire appeared.

This flower stretched like a golden
bridge between two banks, a garland
that joined our lives and our destiny forever.
Lord, such was love and its prodigies,
rivers, emeralds, and illusions.
Glory to you, incandescent furnace of love!

Time passed, and in the confused splendor
of the passing years
the garland lost its freshness,
and frost encircled the flame
and shadowed the routine;
without us being aware
a curse invaded our lives,
and love began to hibernate.

Lord, fountain of love,
on our knees
we offer our fervent plea;
Be light and fire in our home,
bread, rock, dew,
and backbone.

May each night bind our wounds
and each morning may love rise again
like a renewed spring.
Without you our dreams will be scattered.
Grant us faithfulness, cheerfulness,
and stability.

Maintain the blaze of love
in our home, Lord,
high as the stars
and may unity, as a bounteous river,
travel through our arteries
day after day.

Be the golden link, Lord,
that keeps our lives
incorruptibly intertwined
till the end and beyond. Amen.

22. A Child Is Born

He is here,
and the house is full of fragrance.
One would think spring is here.
In you, most holy Father,
the bounteous source of all fatherhood,
in you are all our resources.
You have sent us a present
longed for and dreamt of:
a child has joined our banquet.
Welcome.

What words could declare our gratitude,
Lord of life?
Thank you for his eyes and his hands,
thank you for his feet and his skin,
thank you for his body and his soul.

We place him in your tender hands.
Please watch over him, and cuddle him,
and fill him with sweetness.

Beloved Father, most holy One,
assign an angel to protect
this child from illness and all evil
on the road to health and well being
to make him mindful of your voice.

And may good, peace, and blessings
be with this child all the days of his life.
Amen.

23. *A Happy Home*

Lord Jesus, you live in a happy family.
Make this house the abode of your presence,
a warm and joyful home.
Send peace upon all its members,
serenity upon our nerves,
control upon our tongues,
health upon our bodies.

May our children be loved
and may they sense it,
and may ingratitude and greed
be banned.
Lord, flood the heart of parents
with patience and understanding
and with unlimited generosity.

Lord God, extend a tent of love
to protect and refresh,
to warm and to nurture
the children of the house.

Give us our daily bread,
and banish from our house
the need to show off,
to shine and to be seen;
free us from the vanities of the world
and from ambitions which make us uneasy
and steal our peace.

May joy shine in our eyes,
may confidence open all doors,
may happiness radiate like the sun,
and may peace be queen of this home.
We ask this of you,
you who were a happy son,
close to Mary and Joseph,
in your home of Nazareth.

24. Good News

At dawn a messenger came,
and in the afternoon the letter carrier.
And the house was filled with light.
Our fears ceased to exist.
And we were able to breathe again.
The most optimistic calculations
were surpassed.

Harmony returned.
Success smiled.
Health was regained.

The good news of the afternoon
filled us with peace.
Smiles reappeared on our lips.
We are happy.

My God, let me say:
sheaves of grain and mountain peaks,
snow and rivers
give thanks to the Lord. Amen.

25. *Requiem for a Loved One*

Silence and peace.
He was taken to the land of life.
Why ask questions?
His home, for now, is rest,
and his clothing, light. Forever.
Silence and peace. What do we know?

My God, Lord of history and master
of yesterday and of tomorrow, in your hands
lie the keys of life and of death.
Without asking us, you have taken him

to your holy dwelling. We close our eyes,
we bow our head, and we simply say: Amen.

Silence and peace.

The music of life has been submerged
in deep waters, and nostalgia rests
in boundless prairies.

The battle is over. He will no longer
know tears. The sun will forever shine
upon him, and peace will determine
his boundaries.

Lord of life and master of our destinies,
in your hands we silently place
our dearly beloved who has left us.

While we entrust his remains to the soil,
may his immortal soul live eternally
in unending peace, in your loving bosom,
Father of mercy.

Silence and peace.

IV. STATE OF MIND

26. *In Times of Fear*

Lord, there are clouds on the horizon
and the sea is in a fury.
I am frightened!

Fear paralyzes my blood.
Invisible hands pull me back,
I have no courage!

A flock of dark birds is crossing
the firmament.
What is this?

My God, tell my soul "I am your victory."

Repeat within me:
"Do not fear, I am with you."

27. *Peace*

Lord, fill my heart with hope
and my lips with sweetness!

Fill my eyes with the light
that embraces and purifies.

Mark my hands with a forgiving touch.
Give me courage in my struggles,
compassion when offended,
mercy in ungratefulness and injustice.

Deliver me from envy
and from petty ambition,
from hatred and vengeance,
and as I return tonight to my rest,
may I feel your presence within me.
Amen.

28. *Times of Depression*

My God, my God, why have you forsaken me?
I feel as if a brick wall had unexpectedly
collapsed on me. I do not know where to run,
I do not want to live. Where are you, Lord?

Wretched, in a waste land, I see only shadows
around me. Where can I go? God, have mercy.

Poor wingless angel! Forsaken on misty roads.
Where am I? I am at the bottom of the sea

and I cannot breathe. Where is the light? Does the sun still shine?

Worse than emptiness and nothingness, what is this horror of being simply human?
My God, why do you not remove me from the land of the living?

Like a besieged city, anguish, dejection, bitterness and torment encircle and suffocate me. What is this called? Nausea? Aversion to life? Desolation stretches its grey wings from horizon to the next. Where is the way out? Is there no exit? You alone are my refuge, my God.

I do not forget, Jesus, Son of God and servant of the Father, that at Gethsemane, under the shadows of the olive trees and in the moon-light, tedium and agony made you shed tears and blood; and I remember that an intense and deadly sadness flooded your inner being like a bitter sea. But everything passed.

I know that my night shall also pass. I know you will remove this darkness, my God, and that tomorrow solace will awaken. The massive barrier will collapse and I shall breathe once more. Tomorrow my poor soul will be cared for and I shall live anew.

And I shall say: thank you my God, because this was all a nightmare; the bad dream of a night that now belongs to the past. Meanwhile, give me patience and hope. Your will be done, my God. Amen.

29. Gratitude

Even if our lips were filled with songs
like the sea,
and our tongue filled with joy
like the lap of its waves,
our lips overflowing with praise
like the infinity of the firmament;
and even if our eyes glowed
like the sun and the moon,
and our arms stretched out
like an eagle into space,
and our feet were as weightless
as deers'...

We could not begin to thank you,
our God and God of our fathers,
nor to bless your name for what you have done

for our forefathers and for us.
Amen.

30. *Forgive Me, Lord*

If, exhausted, I fall in the middle of the road,
forgive me, Lord.
If one day my heart staggers
at the thought of suffering,
forgive me, Lord.

Forgive my weakness.
Forgive my hesitation.

The splendid garland
I offered to God this morning
is already withering;
its beauty vanishes.
Forgive me, Lord.

V. SELF-SURRENDER

31. *Act of Abandonment*

In your hands, Oh God, I abandon myself.
Mold this clay as the potter does.
Give it shape, and afterward,
if you so wish, break it.
Command, order.
"What do you want me to do?
What do you want me to avoid?"

Praised or humiliated, persecuted,
misunderstood or slandered,
comforted, hurt, useless,
following your Mother's example,
the only thing for me to say is:
"Let it be done unto me
according to your word."

Give me love; above all things,
love for the cross.
Not of a heroic cross
that would satisfy my ego,
but the humble everyday crosses

which I shoulder reluctantly.
Give me the love for those crosses
that I encounter each day
in contradiction, in neglect, in failure,
in erroneous judgements and in indifference;
in rebuff and contempt from others,
in discomfort and in sickness,
in intellectual limitations and
in barrenness, in the silence of the heart.

Only then will you know that I love you,
even though I may not know it myself.
But that will be enough. Amen.

32. *Surrender*

The road that leads to a friend
is never too long,
nor too small the place
where he lives.
If generous individuals
follow the road which leads to you
and earnestly request of you
the gifts of the spirit,
one after another.

We, on the contrary,
leave our mounts
in total surrender to your will,
and refuse to continue
the journey in which we stop unceasingly
to start anew.
We leave our impediments
before your door.

My God, without exception,
we entrust to you all our interests.

Dispose of them as you wish;
do not let us go back to our own securities,
God of Majesty! Amen.

33. *Prayer of Surrender*

My Father,
I surrender myself to you:
do with me what you will.
Whatever you do,
I thank you for it.

I am ready for everything,
and I accept everything,
provided that your will be done in me

and in all your creatures.
I desire nothing else, Oh my God.

I entrust my soul into your hands.
I give it to you, my God,
with all the love of my heart,
because I love you,

and it is a necessity to love you,
to surrender myself to you, to entrust myself
into your hands without measure,
with infinite confidence,
for you are my Father. Amen.

34. Patience

Child,
if you seriously decide to venture
on the road to God,
prepare your soul
for the trials that will occur,
sit patiently before his doorstep,
calmly accepting the silence,
absence and delays
to which he will submit you,
for gold is refined in the hearth.

Since you lived among us, Lord Jesus,
clothed with patience as a distinctive sign,
Patience is the queen of virtues
and the most precious jewel of your crown.

Give me the grace to peacefully accept
the intrinsic gratuity of God,
the bewildering road of grace,
and the unpredictable emergencies
of nature.

I calmly agree to follow
the slow and staggering pace of prayer,
and I accept that the road to holiness
is so long and difficult.

I accept with peace
life's displeasures
and the lack of understanding from others,
sickness and death itself,
and the law of human insignificance.
That is to say that, after my death,
all will continue as before.

I peacefully accept the fact of wanting
so much and being capable of so little,
and that with great efforts
I will obtain only minimal results.

I peacefully accept the law of sin. That is:
I do what I do not want to do,
and I do not do what I would like to do.
In peace, I leave in your hands
what I should have been and was not,
and what I should have done and did not.

I accept in peace all the human incapacities
which surround me and restrict me.
I peacefully accept the law of perils
and of what is provisional,
the law of mediocrity and of failure,
the law of solitude and of death.
In exchange for this surrender,
Lord, give me peace.

35. *Take Me*

Take me, Lord Jesus,
take me with all that I am,
with all that I have and all that I achieve,
with what I think and what I live.
Take my spirit,
so that it may cling to you
in the intimacy of my heart
and love only you.

My God, take me in my secret desires,
so that they may be my dreams
and my ultimate goal,
my only aspiration and
my perfect happiness.

Take me with your goodness;
attract me to you.
Take me with your gentleness;
accept me in you.
Take me with your love;
unite me to you.
Take me my Savior, in your suffering,
your joy, your life, your death,
in the night of your cross,
in the everlasting day of your resurrection.

Take me with your power; lift me to you;
take me with your fire; set me ablaze;
take me with your greatness,
so that I may lose myself in you.

Take me for the work of your great mission,
so that I may surrender myself completely to
the salvation of my fellows, men and women,
and to any sacrifice at their service.

Take me, oh Christ, my God,
without limitations and without end.

Take whatever I can offer you;
never give back to me what you have taken,
so that one day
I may possess you in heaven,
hold you and keep you forever. Amen

36. *Hymn of Abandonment*

My Father,
today I lift my voice in song to you,
because, instead of daylight,
in lieu of the sun with its light and colors,
you have left me in the darkness
of the cold night.

I love you,
I adore you,
because the waves of the sea of your might
have flooded and destroyed
my dreams and my castles;
they have undone the sweetest,
the strongest,
the most sacred links of my existence.

I love you,
I adore you, and I bless you,
because instead of the warmth

of your tenderness,
the coldness of indifference
entered my garden, freezing every last flower.

Lord, my God,
I bless you and praise you,
for in your most holy will
you have permitted the shadows of dusk
to fade the richness of my youth;
because you wanted me to be, not
a star nor a brilliant and lovely chalice,
but plain and trivial sand
in the vast beach of humanity.

If one day I praised you in joy
and sang to you in the heart of this light
with which you have transfigured my life,
today I love and adore you
in the shadow of the cross.

I bless you in difficulty and in work,
amidst the stones and the ruggedness
of the ascent;
and the tears I shed today
fall from my grateful soul
that blessed you in tedium and poverty,
in the gray shadows of sadness,
because in spite of it all

you affectionately gave me
this infinite and blue vault
to shroud, Lord, my misfortune.

Yes, I kiss affectionately
and in self-surrender
these divine hands that hurt me.
It is because I firmly believe
that neither one hair nor one leaf drops
without the loving will of the Father
who conducts the vast orchestra
of the universe.

Yes, powerful and beloved Father,
my astonished and grateful soul
praises you from deep within,
and I exult in a song of hope.
If one day you changed my plans,
if for one moment you put out my flame,
it was because beyond the glimmer of objects,
of perfumes, of flowers that wither,
I catch sight of another world,
different and more beautiful,
a homeland where the sun does not set,
and a luminous house built on eternal peace.
I place myself in your hands;
do with me what you will. Amen.

VI. TRANSFORMATION

37. The Grace of Fraternal Love

Lord Jesus,
it was your great dream:
that we be one as you and the Father,
and that our unity be fulfilled in your unity.

It was your great commandment, your last will
and distinctive banner for those who follow
you: that we love one another as you loved
us; and you loved us as the Father loved you.
That was the source and magnitude of the
model.

With twelve, you made a family of pilgrims.
You were truthful and sincere with them,
demanding and understanding, but most of all
you were very patient.

Just as in a family,
you warned them against dangers,
you encouraged them
in difficult times

you rejoiced in their success,
you washed their feet,
you served them at the table.
First you gave us the example
and then you gave us the command:
Love one another as I have loved you.

In this new family or fraternity which we belong to today, your are a gift from the Father, and we accept you as our brother. Lord Jesus, you will be strength and the joy which bind us together.

If you are not living among us, this community will collapse like an artificial structure.

You renew yourself and come to life in each member, and for this reason we strive to respect each other as we would respect you; and your presence will question us when unity and peace are threatened in our midst. Therefore, we ask that you remain very much alive within our hearts.

Tear down the high walls of selfishness, pride and vanity that stand between us. Keep away from our doors the envies which obstruct and destroy unity. Deliver us of inhibitions. Calm aggressive impulses. Purify our original sources. And allow us to feel as you felt and to love as you loved. You will be our model and guide, Oh Lord Jesus.

Give us the grace of fraternal love: may a sensible, warm, and deep current run through our relationships; may we understand and forgive each other; may we encourage and enjoy each other as sons and daughters of the same mother. Do not allow obstacles, withdrawals nor blockages in our path, but rather let us all be open, loyal, sincere, and loving, so that trust may grow like a shady tree to cover us all, brothers and sisters in one home, Lord Jesus Christ.

Thus we will achieve a warm, happy home which will rise as a city on a mountain, as a prophetic sign that your Great Dream has been attained and that you, Lord Jesus, are alive among us. Amen.

38. Decision

Oh, Christ,
I am in the darkness,

and the darkness hurts
and injures me.
I miss you.
I know you are in me.
But you are quiet, still
awaiting my decision.

You know
I cannot live without you.
Life without you is empty,
it has no meaning,
it is colorless.
It is agony.

Oh Christ,
do not stay silent.
Save me!

39. *True Conversion*

I know you are asking for something from me,
Lord Jesus.
So many doors open at once;
my life is before my eyes,
not as in a dream.

I know you expect something of me, Lord,
and here I am

at the foot of the wall: everything is open,
there is only one free road,
open to the infinite, to the absolute.

But in spite of everything,
I have not changed. I will still seek you, Lord,
for a long time.
Then, to die, but this time for good.

Like the wounded who suffer, Lord,
I ask that you put an end to my struggle.
I am tired of not belonging to you
and of not being Yours.

40. Be Still

How good it is to pause!
Lord, I would like to slow down
right now.
Why so much commotion?
Why so much frenzy?
I do not know how to stop.
I have forgotten to pray.
Now I close my eyes and
wish to talk to you, Lord.
I wish to open up myself to your universe,
but my eyes cannot bear to stay closed.

I feel a frantic agitation
invade my entire body;
it comes and goes, a prisoner of haste.
Lord, I would like to stop right now.
Why such a hurry?
Why such unrest?
I cannot save the world.

I am merely a drop of water
in the immense ocean
of your marvelous creation.
What is really important
is to seek your presence.
What is really important
is to stop from time to time,
and to proclaim
your greatness,
your beauty, your splendor,
and your love.
What is urgent is to listen to you
and to let you speak within me,
to live in the depth of things
and to take the time to look
constantly for you in the
silence of your mystery.

My heart continues to beat,
but in a different way.

I am doing nothing,
I am not hurrying,
I am simply before you, Lord.
And how good it is to be before you. Amen.

41. *The Grace of Humility*

Lord Jesus, meek and humble.

From the dust I feel controlled by this unquenchable thirst to be admired. The need to be loved by others oppresses me. My heart is full of impossible dreams.

I crave for redemption.
My God, have mercy.

I simply cannot forgive;
resentment consumes me,
criticism hurts me,
failure devastates me,
rivalry frightens me.

My heart is conceited. Give me the grace of humility, my Lord, gentle and meek of heart.

I do not know the origin of this insane appetite to impose my will, to eliminate any rival, to consent to vengeance. I do what I do not want to do. Have mercy, Lord, and give me the grace of humility.

Enormous chains encircle my heart; this heart subdues and takes over all that I am and all that I do, everything that surrounds me. And these appropriations generate so many fears in me. Poor me, owner of myself, who will break my chains? Your grace, my poor and humble Lord. Give me the grace of humility.

The grace to forgive with all my heart. The grace to accept criticism and contradiction, or at least the grace to doubt myself when I am corrected.

Give me the grace of self-criticism.

The grace to remain undisturbed by scorn, neglect, and indifference; to feel happiness in being unknown; to discourage feelings, words, and actions of self-satisfaction.

Lord, open free spaces in me so that they may be filled by you and my brothers and sisters.

Then, my Lord Jesus Christ, give me the grace to acquire an unattached and open heart like yours; a meek and patient heart. Christ Jesus, gentle and meek, make my heart like yours. Amen.

42. Before Your Face, Lord

I have looked for you, Lord, as much as I could, as much as you allowed me. I have done my utmost to understand with my intellect what I believed through faith. I challenged and became extremely tired.

Lord, my God, my only hope, listen to me so that I may not become disheartened and cease to seek you. I have always strived to see your face. Give me strength for the quest. You allowed me to find you and gave me the hope of a better understanding. Before you are my strength and my feebleness; keep the first and heal the latter. Before you are my wisdom and my ignorance. If you open your door, welcome those who enter, and if you close it, open it for those who knock insistently.

Make me remember you, make me understand and love you. Make these gifts grow in me until the moment I surrender to you completely. Amen.

43. The Grace of Mutual Respect

Jesus Christ, our Lord and our brother,
place a bolt on the door of our heart
so that it may not think evil of anyone,
judge unfavorably,
make false assumptions or misinterpret;
so that we may not invade
the sacred sanctuary of intentions.

Lord Jesus, unifying link of our fraternity, put
a seal of silence on our lips in order to block
any murmuring or unfavorable comment, to
zealously keep confidences until death,
knowing that the first and most perfect way
to love is to keep silence.

Make us kind and understanding. Give us a
spirit of courtesy so that we may have for one
another the consideration we would have for
you. And at the same time, give us the
necessary wisdom to surround this courtesy
with fraternal trust.

Lord Jesus Christ, give us the grace
to respect one another. Amen.

44. Lead Me

Guide me, radiant light,
through the darkness that surrounds me;
lead me always further on.
This night is dark
and I am far from home;
guide me further on.

Guide my steps: I do not ask
to see right away
what you have in store for me.
One step at a time is sufficient
for the time being.
I was not always like this,
and I have not always prayed
for you to lead me.
I preferred my own way;
but now I pray that you will guide me.
I dreamed of days of glory,
and pride lead my steps.
I pray: do not remember those past years.

Your might has blessed me abundantly;
and today you will undoubtedly lead me
through mounts and vales,
through stony paths and steep ridges,

until night ends
and morning smiles.
Tomorrow, the faces of angels
I loved for so long,
but have lost sight of,
will smile again.

Guide me, radiant light,
lead me farther. Amen.

45. *The Gift of Dialogue*

Lord God, we praise you and glorify you for
the beauty of the gift named *dialogue*. It is a
favorite child of God, for it is like a stream
unceasingly gushing within the Holy Trinity.

Dialogue unties knots,
dissipates suspicions,
opens doors,
resolves conflicts,
makes persons greater.
It is the bond of unity
and the "mother" of brotherhood.

Christ Jesus, unity of the gospel community,
make us realize that our lack of understanding
is almost always due to a lack of dialogue.

Make us understand that dialogue is neither an argument nor a battle of ideas, but a search for the truth between two or more people. Make us understand that we need each other, and that we complement each other: we have something to give and a need to receive; I can see what others cannot, and they can see what I do not.

Lord Jesus, when tension builds up, give me humility so that I will not want to impose my truth by attacking my brother's truth; make me keep silence when necessary; make me wait for the other person to finish expressing his truth completely.

Give me wisdom to understand that no human being is able to completely possess the truth, and that no error or tactlessness is without some truth.

Give me common sense to recognize that I can also be mistaken on one or another aspect of truth; let me be enriched by the other person's truth. Finally, give me the generosity to understand that the other person also seeks the truth honestly and to accept the opinion

of others without prejudice and with kindness.
Lord Jesus, give me the gift of dialogue. Amen.

46. Transfiguration

Lord, we are together again.
Together, you and I,
and you and my brothers and sisters.
Your life has entered my life.

My history is so trite, so empty,
so common.
I do not even have a history.

Sometimes I wonder
if my life has any meaning.
So much emptiness, so many complications,
so much unfaithfulness!

But when I am with you,
it is as if enthusiasm
and energy came back to life.

And today with my brothers
Peter, James and John,
I saw your face transfigured,
glowing.

You, Lord Jesus, are the God of all light.
You are the God of brightness and beauty.

It is good to be close to you,
it is good to live with you.
But Lord, it is even better
to know that you are with me
throughout my life,
by your grace, by your love.
It is good to know,
as you transform me, that my face
will also be transfigured, glowing.

Freely, cheerfully,
with joy I beseech you that I may
be more and more identified with you,
to the point of saying,
with the apostles,
"Master, it is good to be here!"

47. The Grace of Communication

Lord Jesus,
you have called the disciples "friends",
because you revealed
your innermost self to them.
How hard it is to open oneself, Lord!

How difficult it is to tear apart
the veil of one's own mystery.

How many obstacles are on the road!
But I know very well, Lord,
that without communication
there is no love,
and that the essential mystery of fraternity
consists of unveiling and of welcoming
one another.

Make me understand, Lord,
that I was created,
not as a complete and closed being,
but to grow and move
toward others;
that I must share in the richness of others
and let them share in my richness,
that to close oneself is death,
and to open oneself is life,
freedom, maturity.

Lord Jesus Christ, king of fraternity,
give me the confidence and the courage
to open myself to others;
teach me the art of unveiling myself.
Destroy the shyness and fear in me,
the barriers and restraints

that are obstacles to the flow
of communication.
Give me the generosity to spring forward
without fear into the rewarding game
of opening and welcoming.

Lord Jesus,
give us the grace of communication.

VII. APOSTOLIC WORK

48. In the Likeness of Jesus

Lord Jesus,
may your presence overwhelm my being,
and your likeness be engraved
in my heart,
so that I may walk in the light of your face,
think as you thought,
feel as you felt,
behave the way you behaved,
talk as you talked,
dream as you dreamed,
and love as you loved.

That I may, like you,
forget myself
in order to attend to others;
to be insensitive to myself
and compassionate towards others;
to sacrifice myself, and at the same time,
to encourage and give hope to others.

That I may, like you,
be sensitive and merciful,
patient, meek and humble,
genuine and true.
That your favorites, the poor,
may also be my favorites;
your goals become my goals.
That seeing me, other may see you.
And that I may become the transparency
of your being and your love. Amen.

49. *Prayer for Action*

Lord, give us the wisdom
that judges from above and sees from afar.
Give us the spirit that omits
the irrelevant in favor of the essential.
Teach us serenity
in times of confrontation,
teach us to progress in faith without agitation
along the road you laid out.
Give us peace
so that we may embrace everything
with a vision of unity.

Help us to accept criticism
and contradiction.

Let us avoid
disorder and dispersion.

With you, may we love all things.
Oh God, source of being, unite us to you
and to everything that leads us
to happiness and eternity. Amen.

50. *You Are with Us*

You are with us every day
until the end of the world.

You are with us, Divine Omnipotence,
with our frailties.

You are with us, infinite love,
who accompanies us on our way.

You are with us, supreme protection
and guaranteed triumph over temptation.

You are with us, energy that supports
our hesitant generosity.

Your are with us
in our struggles and our failures,
in our difficulties and our trials.

You are with us
in our disappointments and our anxieties,
to grant us courage once more.

You are with us in sadness
to communicate the enthusiasm
of your joy.

You are with us in solitude
like an unwavering friend.

You are with us
in our apostolic mission,
to guide and sustain us.

You are with us
to lead us to the Father
on the road of wisdom
and eternity. Amen.

51. *Solidarity*

You were the first, Christ Jesus, to relinquish
the glory of divinity, to become one with man,
poor pilgrim who bears this solitude. You
participated in the caravan of human existence along with its ultimate consequences.

Bind me to others
so that I may walk with the crippled,
lend a hand to the blind,
assist those who die abandoned in hospitals,
teach reading and writing to the illiterate,
share my house with the homeless,
who have been evicted for not paying the rent,
help whoever has an extreme emergency,
protest in the name of those
who have been tortured
or massacred for defending the oppressed,
take the bread from my mouth to give it
to the hungry dying on the road,
attend the funerals of those who died in factory
accidents, on the scaffolds, in any field
of work, or those who fell in the streets,
riddled with bullets by agents of oppression.

Take the place of one who has raised
his voice in favor of the oppressed,
be part of the march of those who fight
for human rights, for the unity of workers,
for better wages, for brotherly understanding,
for justice, and for peace.

They will all sit by your right hand, Lord,
haloed by the beatitudes; those persecuted for
justice, and those who worked for peace.

52. Prayer of Petition

Give me, Lord, the candor of a child
and the conscience of an adult.
Give me, Lord, the caution of an astronaut
and the courage of a rescuer.
Give me, Lord, the humbleness of a sweeper
and the forbearance of the sick.

Give me, Lord, the idealism of youth
and the wisdom of old age.
Give me, Lord, the willingness
of the Good Samaritan
and the gratitude of the needy.
Give me, Lord, all the good that I see
in my brothers and my sisters,
whom you have overwhelmed
with your gifts.

Lord, let me imitate your saints;
or better still, make me
what you want me to be:
persevering like a fisherman,
hopeful like a Christian.

Let me remain on the path of your Son
and at the service of my brothers and sisters.
Amen.

53. *Generosity*

Lord, teach me how to be generous,
to give without speculating,
to repay evil with good,
to serve without expecting a reward,
to get close to those who least please me,
to do good to those who cannot repay me,
to love freely always,
to work without seeking rest.

And while having nothing to give
but generosity,
to give myself always more
to whomever needs me,
expecting the reward from you alone.
Or better still: hoping you,
yourself, will be my reward.
Amen.

54. *Where Are You?*

I beseech you, Lord, that I may one day
hear the song of men and women
who have found love,
and see the day when they will have forgotten
hatred, wars, races, colors.

One day, I hope to see a new world
rediscover its faith in you.

For you alone can fulfill
the emptiness felt by the world.

I also look for you.
Where are you? Where...
Where are you?
When night falls upon earth,
I turn to you.
But the stars do not answer
my questions.

I know you are in my brothers and my sisters.
I know their voice is your voice.
I know your skin is of every color.
I know you speak every language.
I know you are in all nations.
I know your name knows no limits
of time or space.

I have looked for you, and now I know
where you are. Amen.

55. *The Grace of Work*

Since early childhood, Lord Jesus,
you earned your bread
by the sweat of your brow
in the shop of an artisan.
Since then, work has acquired a divine nobility.

Through work, we are transformed
into companions and cooperators of God
and into craftsmen of our history.
Work is the anvil with which man shapes
his maturity and his grandeur,
the flour with which daily bread is made.

Matter, passing through the hands of men,
is transformed into a vehicle of love.
Make me understand, Lord,
the love of those who build shelters,
those who sow grain,
those who sweep streets,
build houses, repair damages,
listen to problems,

or simply prepare themselves
for tomorrow's labor and service.

Give us, Lord, the grace to offer you
the day's labor as a liturgical gesture,
as a living mass dedicated to your glory
and the service of our brothers and sisters.
Amen.

56. *Word and Fire*

Father, fountain of life and warmth, send us
your living word; let us greet it without fear,
and let us be embraced by it.

Let your word come, Lord, and when our
hearts are aflame with your unquenchable fire,
we will transmit this fire to one another.

Transform us, Lord, into warm and glowing
words, able to set the world on fire, so that
each person may feel wrapped in the infinite
flames of your love. Amen.

57. We Pray to You, Lord

Lord God, we ask you to bless the honest work done in fields and factories; in schools, offices and stores; in any place where we earn our daily bread for the development of art and science.

And since you commanded humans to control and to master the forces of creation, lead us by the hand, Lord, so that we may use natural energy, especially the ones over which we have some control, for the good of people and not for their destruction, thanking you, Lord and creator of all the forces of the universe.

Since you have given us such marvelous power, make all people, brothers and sisters, recognize you in Jesus Christ, Lord and Redeemer of all creatures, and may we serve you with a deep sense of responsibility in each of the actions we undertake.

Have mercy on men and women who do not have hope, and on those who, day after day, experience only suffering. Lord, we implore you: stay with us, through your word, by your grace, and by the solace of the Holy Spirit. In

the name and by the merits of Jesus Christ,
savior and hope of the world. Amen.

58. *Option for the Poor*

Lord Jesus, brother of the poor,
before the dubious glitter of the powerful
you stripped yourself of your power.

From the heights of divinity
you came down toward us
and touched our abyss.

Being all richness you became poverty.
Being the center of the world,
you became its outskirts,
limited and captive.

You left aside the rich and the satisfied,
and you took the torch
of the oppressed and the forsaken,
and you stood by their side.
Lifting high the banner of mercy,
you walked through heights and vales,
searching for the injured sheep.

You said the rich already had their god
and that only the poor are still capable

of amazement;
for them the land and the kingdom,
the field and the harvest will be theirs.
Blessed are they!
It is time to fold our tents and move on,
to stop misfortune and lament,
to break chains
and to continue our struggle for dignity,
so that the dawn of liberation
may come at last,
when swords are buried
in the fertile soil.

There are many poor, Lord; they are legion.
Like a swelling storm, their hue and cry bursts,
grows, impetuous and sometimes threatening.

Give us, Lord Jesus, your sensitive
and daring heart;
free us from indifference and passivity;
enable us to get involved,
to take a stand also
for the poor and the destitute.

Time has come to collect the banners
of righteousness and of peace,
to get deeply involved with the masses,
between tension and conflict,

and with alternative solutions
to defy materialism.

Give us, king of the poor,
the wisdom to weave a single garland
with these two red flowers:
contemplation and combat.
And give us the crown of the beatitudes.
Amen.

59. *To Serve*

Oh Christ, give me a noble heart
to better serve you.
A heart that is strong enough
to aspire to great ideals
and not to mediocre options.

A heart that is generous at work,
viewing it not as an imposition,
but rather as a mission you entrust me with.

A heart that is noble in suffering,
a brave soldier before its own cross,
helping others to carry theirs.

A heart that is open to the world,
understanding its frailty,
but immune to its maxims and seductions.

A heart that is generous and open
towards men and women,
loyal and attentive toward all,
but especially obliging and dedicated
toward the poor and the humble.

A heart that is never self-centered,
but always dependent on you,
happy to serve you
and to serve my brethren,
my Lord,
all the days of my life. Amen.

VIII. MARY

60. *Lady of Silence*

Mother of silence and humility,
you who are lost and found
in the mystery of the Lord.

You are availability and receptivity.
You are fertility and plenitude.
You are attention and tender care
towards all.
You are clothed in fortitude.

Human maturity
and spiritual elegance are alive in you.
You are your own mistress
before being our lady.

There is no dispersal in you.
In a simple and total act,
your motionless soul
is identified with the Lord.
You are in God and God is on you.
Total mystery encompasses
and penetrates you,

possesses, dwells in,
and integrates your whole being.

It seems as if everything
has remained motionless in you,
has been identified with you:
time, space, word,
music, silence, woman, God.
Everything in you seems
to have been assumed and deified.

No one has ever seen
such a gentle human image,
and no one will ever see on earth
a woman interceding so lovingly.

Nevertheless,
your silence is not absence but presence.
You are lost in the Lord,
and at the same time,
attentive to all of us, as in Cana.

Never is communication so profound
as when no word is uttered,
and never is silence as eloquent
as when nothing is said.

Make us understand that silence
is not a lack of interest in others,

but a radiant source of energy
that unfolds;
and to overflow
one must be filled.

The world drowns
in the sea of dispersion,
and it is impossible to love one's brethren
with a dispersed heart.
Make us understand that,
as apostles, we must love silence,
but that silence
without acts of mercy is nothing but comfort.

Cover us with the cloak of your silence,
and give us the strength of your faith,
the heights of your hope,
the depth of your love.
Remain with those who stay,
and go with those who leave.
Oh admirable Mother of silence!

61. *When I Am Weary*

Mother, I come from the turmoil of life, I am
exhausted, body and soul.

It is hard to accept peacefully what happens around us in a day of work and struggle. The things we had put so much hope in betray us. People to whom we wish to be kind resist us. And those from whom we seek help try to take advantage of us.

This is why I come to you, Mother, because deep inside me lives an insecure child. But close to you I feel strong and full of confidence. Only the thought of having a mother such as you gives me courage. I feel that your arm supports me and that your hand guides me. I can thus continue on my way undisturbed.

Renew me entirely, so that I may see the beauty of life. Lift me so that I may walk without fear. Give me your hand so that I may always find my way. Bless me so that my presence in the world may be a sign of your blessing. Amen.

62. Our Lady of Eastertide

Lady of Eastertide,
Lady of Friday and Sunday,
Lady of night and morning,

Lady of silence and of the cross,
Lady of love and surrender,
Lady of the word received
and of the word pledged,
Lady of peace and of hope.

Lady of every departure,
because you are the Lady
of the "passage" or of "passover", hear us.
Today, we wish to "thank you."
Thank you, our Lady for your "fiat,"
for your availability as a servant,
for your poverty and your silence,
for the suffering of your seven swords,
for the joy of your departures,
which brought peace to so many.
Thank you very much
because you have remained with us
in spite of time and distance.

Our Lady of reconciliation,
image and origin of the church;
today we place in your
silent and accessible heart
this pilgrim church of Easter.

A church essentially missionary,
leaven and soul of society

in which we live,
a prophetic church, proclamation
of the kingdom which is already here.

A church of authentic witnesses,
inserted in the human history
as the saving presence of the Lord,
source of peace, of joy, and of hope. Amen.

63. *Praise to God*

You alone are holy, Lord God,
you who do wonders.
You are strong, you are great,
you are most high,
you are good, all good, supreme good,
Lord God, living and true.
You are charity and love, you are wisdom.
You are humility, you are patience,
you are protection,
you are peacefulness, you are well-being,
you are joy,
you are beauty, you are meekness.
You are our protector,
our guardian and our defender.
You are our strength and our hope.

You are sweetness.
You are our eternal life,
great and admirable Lord.

64. *New Psalm of Creation* (Fragments)

Allow us to praise you, oh God,
in all the worlds you have created.

Allow us to praise you
on the heights where angels abide.

Allow us to praise you
in the depths of the glistening stars.

Allow us to praise you, our God,
at the foot of the angel
who closes the gates of hell.

Allow us to praise you, oh God,
with the twittering,
noisy and multicolored birds
that delight our eyes and ears.

Allow us to praise you, oh God,
for nests in the trees,
where fledglings lift
their bare necks
toward their mother who brings them food.

Allow us to praise you, oh God,
with mighty birds
that fly over the seas
and take wing towards
perpetual snows.

Allow us to praise you, oh God,
for the animals of the earth,
big and small, full of tenderness
or overflowing with indomitable force.
Do not allow them to be extinguished,
but let them live.

And may new generations arrive
to praise you.

Allow us to praise you, oh God,
Trinity in one, for the animals of the earth
with nimble feet,
and most pleasant to behold.
Do not let them perish
because of great and powerful animals
that crush everything.
The large animal also has a heart,
and little ones to protect.

Allow us to praise you
in the roundness of the earth,

for everything that flies and runs,
swims and arises from the deep.

All things belong to you:
your finger is pouring out
beauty everywhere,
in multicolored feathers and in claws,
in the strength of the winds.

Your love is unfathomable
and impenetrable everywhere.

Small animals are born everywhere,
defenseless and blind,
seeking their mother's milk.

Blessed are you, one God and Trinity,
for the splendid rocks
of mountains and glaciers.

Blessed are you for cascades
and mighty rivers,
for calm waters,
deep and silent.
Receive praise, with much affection,
for small springs
that provide water so that fish may live.

Praised are you, my God,
for storms
on earth and sea,

for sand storms
in the deserts.

Blessed are you, glorious God,
for the splendor of millions
of scented flowers with beautiful shapes.
This blossoming is never ending
and cannot be annihilated.
And even if you send a disaster
to land, it never lasts long;
and a new spring bursts forth;
and a new magnificence
governs the earth.

Allow us to praise you, oh God,
for your angels.
They are powerful and admirable to behold.
They are servants of your will;
they combat for your word
and humbly submit themselves
to your command.

Wonderful and eternal is your holy desire
to edify people and more.
And even if they fail,
if they kneel before you
like prodigal children
you bend over them

with patience and kindness,
telling them: Come, children,
return to original innocence
and I shall welcome you
as a father greets his children.

Your patience towards people is immense,
oh God, eternal and excellent.

Nonetheless, people do not see it;
they invade fields, trample flowers,
hunt birds and destroy nests.

People fight enslave, imprison,
condemn one another to death.

No one has patience such as yours, my God,
and on earth we will never cease
to address eternal praise to you.

Allow us to adore you, eternally.
Let eternal praise
endure on earth.
As far as our eyes can see,
all is yours, everything belongs to you,
your hand is upon every creature.

Be glorified and praised,
most holy God,
in each heart you created for your glory.

You want to be with us eternally,
most holy God.
You, three times holy, praiseworthy;
you, our beatitude.
Oh, three times holy,
three times admirable,
three times divine, ineffable God. Amen.

65. *Face to Face*

Day after day, Lord of my life,
may I remain before you,
face to face.
With clasped hands,
I will stay before you,
Lord of all the worlds,
face to face.

In this world that is yours,
in the midst of exhaustion,
turmoil, conflict; in the midst
of impassioned multitudes,
I must remain before you,
face to face.

And when my duty in this world
is finished,
oh king of kings,
I will remain before you
alone and silent,
face to face. Amen.

TO PRAY

I. PRELIMINARY EXERCISES

Many people do not progress on the path of prayer because they overlook the necessary preparation.

At times, when you wish to pray, you will feel calm. In this case, there is no need to prepare yourself. Just concentrate, invoke the Holy Spirit, and pray.

On other occasions, as you begin to pray, you will feel so nervous and your thoughts will be so scattered, that if you do not first calm down you will not get anywhere.

Something else might occur in that, after many minutes of pleasant prayer, you may find that you are getting tense and preoccupied. If at this particular moment you do not practice a relaxation exercise, not only will you waste time, but this time of prayer will prove unpleasant and counter productive.

Here are a few easy exercises. It is up to you to decide which ones to use, when, for how long, and in what manner. This choice depends on the need and circumstances.

When you wish to pray, always assume a correct body position, with your head and trunk erect. Make sure you can breathe easily. Relax your tensions and nerves; let go of memories and images, empty yourself, and be silent. Concentrate. Place yourself in the presence of God, invoke the Holy Spirit, and begin to pray. Four or five minutes of preparation are sufficient—that is, when you are calm.

Body Relaxation. When you are calm and focused, release all the tension in your legs and arms by stretching and contracting the muscles. Notice how tension disappears. Loosen your shoulders in a similar manner; loosen the muscles of your face and forehead. Relax. Close your eyes. Loosen the muscles and nerves of your neck by moving your head gently to and fro and turning it slowly from one side to the other, calmly and attentively. Feel how your muscles and nerves relax. Take about ten minutes for this exercise.

Mental Silencing. In a very calm and concentrated manner, start repeating the word "peace" in a low voice—if possible, when exhaling—and notice how a soothing peace begins to flood your brain. Take a few minutes to feel how your mind relaxes, and after this go through your whole body, repeating the word "peace", and let yourself be flooded with a pleasant sensation of profound peace.

Afterward, repeat this same exercise with the word "nothing", and feel the sensation of *emptiness-nothing,* first in your brain and then throughout your whole being, until you feel a general sensation of rest and silence. Take ten to fifteen minutes for this exercise.

Concentration. Calmly detect the movement of your lungs—simply perceive it and continue to breathe without thinking about anything. Concentrate on this for about five minutes.

After this, stay calm, quiet and attentive; perceive and let go all noises from your attention: be they far, near, strong, or soft. About five minutes.

Following this, with great calm and attention, perceive your heartbeat and concentrate on it, simply feeling the beats without thinking about anything. Do this for five minutes.

Abdominal Breathing. Relax and be calm. Follow what you are doing attentively: inhale slowly through your nose until your lungs are filled, and exhale through your mouth, slightly opened, until all the air is out. A calm, slow, and deep breathing.

The most relaxed breathing is abdominal: lungs are filled as the abdomen swells, and emptied as the abdomen flattens. All of this occurs simultaneously. Do not force anything. At first perform about ten breathing. With time you will be able to add more.

You must use these exercises freely and with flexibility as time, occasion, etc, permit.

At the beginning, you might not notice the results. But things will gradually improve. Sometimes, the effects will be surprisingly positive. On other occasions, it will be quite the opposite. Such is our unpredictable nature.

Some people say that prayer is a grace and does not depend on methods or exercises. This is a serious error. Life with God is a convergence between grace and nature. Prayer is a grace, yes; but it is also an art, and as such it requires training, method, and pedagogy. If many people are stuck in spiritual mediocrity, it is not because grace fails them, but because of their lack of order, discipline, and patience; in a word, it is because nature fails.

II. PRACTICAL GUIDELINES

1. If you feel sleepy when you pray, stand up with your body straight and your heels together.

2. When you feel incapable of praying, think that this may be a test from God or an emergency of nature. Do not force yourself to "feel." Allow the three angels to accompany you: *Patience*: peacefully accept what you cannot resolve. *Perseverance*: continue to pray even though you may not feel anything. *Hope*: everything comes to an end; tomorrow will be better.

3. Never forget that life with God is a *life of faith*. And faith has nothing to do with feeling, but a lot to do with *knowledge*. It is not emotion, but conviction. It is not evidence, but certainty.

4. In order to pray, a method, order, discipline, and flexibility are needed, for the Holy Spirit blows when least expected.

People become stagnated in prayer because they lack method. He who prays without care becomes a careless person.

5. Do not dream, but hope. A dream vanishes; hope endures. Effort, yes; violence, no. An intense struggle to feel devotion produces mental fatigue and discouragement.

6. Remember that God is gratuity. For this reason, his way of teaching us is bewildering; and for this very reason, there is no human logic to prayer: we think this particular effort should produce these results; this action, this reaction; this cause, this effect. On the contrary, there will usually be no proportion between your efforts in prayer and their "results." This is the way it is and it should be accepted peacefully.

7. Prayer is a relationship with God. Relationship is the movement of mental energies, a movement of adhesion to God. It is therefore normal that emotion or enthusiasm fill the soul. But beware! It is necessary to maintain this emotional state under the control of calmness and serenity.

8. When one prays, divine visitation can occur at any moment: at the beginning, in the middle, or at the end; at any moment or never. In this last case, be careful not to be overcome by discouragement and impatience. On the contrary, relax your nerves, abandon yourself, and continue to pray.

9. You complain: "I pray, but it has no noticeable effects in my life." To receive strength from prayer in life, *First*: synthesize your morning prayer in one sentence—for example: "What would Jesus do in my place?" and recall it in each daily circumstance. *Secondly*: when you experience a setback or a strong ordeal, be aware and remember that you have to feel and act as Jesus would.

10. Do not attempt to change your life; it will be enough to improve it. Do not try to be humble; it will suffice to do humble deeds. Do not endeavor to be virtuous; it is sufficient to perform deeds of virtue. To be virtuous is to act like Jesus.

Do not be frightened by a relapse. Backsliding means that you act according to your negative traits. Whenever you are careless or taken by surprise, you will react according to your negative impulses. This is normal. Be patient. When something comes up, try not to be taken off guard; be watchful, and try to act according to the impulses of Jesus.

11. Be aware that you are capable of very little. I say this to encourage you, so that you will not lose heart due to any backsliding. Remember that to grow in God is an extremely slow process, and full of counter-marches. Accept this in peace. After each relapse, get up and move on.

12. Holiness is being in the Lord; to be so much with him that his image is engraved in the soul; to walk in the light of his image. This is holiness.

13. In order to take the first steps in your relationship with God, while you learn to pray, you may use guidelines 1, 2, and 3, suggested under "Methods" in the following section.

In the worst moments of dispersion or futility, do not waste your time; you can always pray through the methods of written prayer, vocal prayer, and prayerful reading, which follow this section.

III. METHODS

1. Prayerful Reading

Take a written prayer, for example, a psalm or any other prayer, but be careful: this has nothing to do with reading one chapter of the Bible or a theme of meditation. The aim is to pray.

Take a prayerful body position and an inner attitude of prayer. Calm yourself and invoke the Holy Spirit.

Begin reading the prayer slowly, very slowly. While reading try to *experience* what you read. What I mean is that you try to *assume* the meaning of the words you read, to feel "with all your soul", making the sentences you read "yours", concentrating your attention on the content and the meaning of the sentences.

If you find an expression that you feel has great significance, stop immediately. Repeat it several times, and through it, be united with the Lord until you have depleted the richness of the phrase, or until its content floods your soul. Think to yourself that God is like the other shore; in order to be linked to that shore, many bridges are not necessary: one is enough. A single sentence can keep us bound together.

If this does not happen, continue to read very slowly, understand and feel with your heart the meaning of what you have read. Stop once in a while. Go back to repeat and relive the most significant expressions.

If at one point you sense that you can abandon the support of reading, put it aside and let the Holy Spirit fill your inner self with spontaneous and inspired thoughts.

This method is always easy and effective. It helps to take the first steps when one experiences aridity, or simply on those days when one cannot think of anything in particular due to mental dispersion or nervousness.

2. *Meditated Reading*

One must carefully choose a book that does not distract, but rather concentrates—most preferably the Bible. It is good to have a

138

personal knowledge of it, that is, to know where to find themes that are significant to you—for example, on consolation, hope, patience—in order to choose among this material what your soul needs on this particular day. You may also follow the liturgical order, with the help of texts proposed for each day.

It is not recommended to open the Bible at random, or to do so seldomly. In any case, before the beginning of a meditated reading, it is better to know what themes you wish to meditate and in which chapter of the Bible.

Take a correct position. Ask for the aid of the Holy Spirit, and calm yourself.

Begin to read slowly, very slowly. As you read, try to *understand* what you are reading: the meaning of the sentence, its context, and the intention of the sacred author. Here lies the difference between a prayerful reading and a meditated reading: in a prayerful reading, one *takes on and lives* what is being read—this is fundamentally a task of the heart. In a meditated reading, one tries to *understand* what is being read—this is basically an intellectual activity, since one handles concepts: explaining, applying, comparing them, in order to penetrate deeper within the divine life, to develop principles of life, standards of judgement. In other words, a Christian mentality.

Continue to read slowly, in order to comprehend what you read.

If you find an idea which strikes your attention, stop right there; close the book; consider the idea in all possible ways; apply it to your life; draw conclusions.

If it does not happen—or after it does—continue to read in a peaceful, concentrated, and quiet manner.

If one paragraph seems difficult to understand, go back; try to read it again to grasp its meaning; to understand this particular passage in the broader context.

Continue to read slowly and attentively.

If at some point your heart is moved and you are prompted to praise, give thanks or implore, feel free to do so.

If nothing happens, continue to read slowly, understanding and considering what you read.

It is normal and convenient for a meditated reading to end in prayer. Try to do this.

Through meditated reading, it is desirable to find practical criteria to implement in one's daily life.

We strongly suggest that during meditation you always hold a book, especially the Bible, in your hands, although it is not necessary to read during this entire period. Saint Theresa tells us that for fourteen years she was unable to meditate unless she held a book in her hands.

3. Brief Guidelines to Meditate and Live the Word

1. Read slowly, very slowly, pausing frequently.

2. Keep your soul empty, open, and expectant.

3. Read unselfishly: do not try to find something, like doctrines, truths.

4. Read, "listening" to the Lord heart-to-heart, person-to-person, attentively, but with a "passive" attention and without anxiety.

5. Do not force yourself to *understand* intellectually or literally. Do not be preoccupied with finding out "what does *this* mean?" but ask yourself "what is God telling me with this?" Do not devote time on individual sentences that, in some cases, do not have any meaning on their own. Drop them: do not be preoccupied with understanding everything literally.

6. If an expression strikes you, underline it and in the margin write a word that summarizes the strong impression.

7. Remove names—for example, Israel, Jacob, Samuel, Moses, Timothy, and put yours in their place. Realize how God calls you by your name.

8. If the reading does not "say" anything to you, stay untroubled, peaceful. It may well be that on another day the same reading will "say" much; for along with our work, grace is or is not; God's time is not our time. You must always have much patience with the workings of God.

9. Do not struggle to catch and possess the exact doctrinal meaning of the Word, but meditate on it like Mary did. Ruminate on it in your mind and heart, and let it fill you. Become saturated with the vibrations and echoes of God's heart. "Keep" the Word; that is, let it echo in you throughout the whole day.

10. In the psalms, "imagine" what Jesus or Mary felt while pronouncing the same words; place yourself mentally in the heart of Jesus Christ and say these words to God, as Jesus might have done. Pray them in his spirit, with his inner disposition, with his feelings.

11. Put the meditated work into practice frequently in your life: reflect upon what sense and circumstances your criteria included in the Word—God's *mind* must influence and alter our ways of thinking and behaving, for the Word must question the life of the believer; in this manner, God's criteria will become ours, until we become transformed into real disciples of the Lord.

12. In summary: read, savor, ponder, meditate, and practice the Word.

4. *Vocal Prayer*

Take a powerful expression that fills your soul —for example, "my God and my all"—or a simple word like "Jesus", "Lord", or "Father."

Begin to utter it, peacefully and deliberately, in a low voice, every ten or fifteen seconds.

As you say it, try to experience the content of the word. Understand that the content is the Lord himself.

Begin to perceive how the "presence" or "substance" contained in this expression slowly and gently inundates your whole being and your mental energies.

Continue to repeat the expression slowly, leaving more and more silence in between each repetition.

You must always use the same expression.

Variant: When we inhale, our body becomes tense because the lungs are filled. On the contrary, when we exhale, our body relaxes, lets go.

In this variation, take advantage of the exhalation—a natural moment of relaxation—to pronounce these expressions. Thus, both body and soul function in harmony. Concentration is easier, since breathing and blood irrigation are excellent. The results are supremely beneficial to the soul as well as to the body.

5. *Written Prayer*

In this prayer, one writes what he or she would like to say to the Lord.

This may well be the only way to pray in times of emergency, in moments of deep aridity or of acute dispersion, on days when one feels desperate or annoyed.

One of the advantages of this method is to concentrate our attention deeply; it also has the advantage of being useful in future moments of prayer, as you read your own writings.

6. Visual Exercise

One takes an expressive picture, for example an image of Jesus, of Mary, or any other subject, a picture that makes a strong impression, such as peace, gentleness, strength. What is important is that it speaks to you deeply.

Take the picture in your hands and after calming down and invoking the Holy Spirit, stay quiet, simply looking at the picture, first as a whole, then in detail.

Secondly, capture intuitively, attentively, and with serenity the impressions this picture evokes in you. What does this image tell you?

Thirdly, with calmness, transfer yourself to the picture, as if you were this image, or as if you were in it. Respectfully and calmly, make "yours" the impressions this picture arouses in you. Thus, identify yourself mentally with this image. Remain so for a good while, and saturate your soul with the sentiments of Jesus which the picture illustrates. This is how the soul puts on the image of Jesus and shares in his interior disposition.

Finally, with this inner disposition, transfer yourself mentally to your daily life. Imagine difficult situations, and overcome them with Jesus' attitudes. This is the way to embody the image of Jesus in the world.

This exercise is particularly fruitful for those who are naturally imaginative.

7. Prayer of Surrender

This prayer—and attitude—is the most authentic in the Gospel. The most liberating. The most appeasing. No anaesthetic can ease life's sorrows better than saying, "I surrender myself unto you, Lord."

We recommend that you memorize prayer number 33 in this book, and say it as you do "The Lord's Prayer" when you encounter everyday obstacles, big or small.

Put yourself everyday in an attitude of surrender, in the presence of the Father who allows or permits everything. You may use prayer number 33, or a simpler one such as: *Your will be done, in your hands I commend myself.*

It is crucial to completely silence your mind, which tends to rebel. Self-surrender is the homage of silence in faith.

Place everything that annoys you in silence and peace with a prayer: your parents, your bodily features, illnesses, old age, powerlessness and limitations, the negative traits of your personality, persons close to you who upset you, unhappy memories, painful experiences, failures, errors.

It might well be that when you remember them they will hurt. But if you place them in the hands of the Father, peace will enfold you.

8. Prayer of Inner Embrace

Contrary to exercise No. 9 *Adoration in Encounter*, where we go forth and peacefully await, in other words the "I" goes out and is deposited in the "You". In this exercise of inner embrace, I remain quiet and receptive, and the YOU comes to me and I joyfully greet his coming. It is convenient to do this exercise with the resurrected Christ.

We will use the verb *to feel*, not in the sense of being moved, but rather of *perceiving*. Much can be felt without being moved. I feel the cold ground, I feel a headache, I feel heat, I feel sad, with no particular attachment.

With the help of certain phrases—which I will indicate at the end—in faith, begin to welcome Jesus, who rose to life and who makes you rise to life, he who comes into you and fill your life. Feel the resurrected presence of Jesus come into the most hidden corners of your soul while you enunciate the phrases at the end of this exercise. Feel how this presence takes full possession of what you are, of what you think, of what you do. Feel how Jesus takes over your innermost heart. In faith welcome him joyfully, without restraint.

In faith, feel how Jesus touches that wound that hurts you; feel how Jesus takes away the thorn of this oppressing anguish; sense how he relieves you from these fears, and liberates you of resentments. You must notice that these sensations are generally felt in the stomach, as a jab. This is why one speaks of a sword of pain.

After this, leap into life. Accompanied by Jesus and clothed in his likeness, stroll mentally along the places where you live or work. Stand before someone with whom you have clashed. Imagine how Jesus would look at that person. Look at him with the eyes of Jesus. Imagine Jesus' serenity if he had to face this conflict or confront this situation. Imagine all sorts of situations, even the most difficult ones, and let Jesus act through you: look through the eyes of Jesus, speak through his mouth. Let his appearance be your appearance. It is not you who lives, but Jesus who lives through you.

This is a transforming or "christifying" exercise.

Take a powerful position, the same as in the exercise *Adoration in Encounter*. After having vocalized and lived the phrase, remain still and silent for a while. Let the meaning of these words resound throughout and fill your soul:

Jesus, come within me.
Take possession of my whole being.
Take me with all that I am,
that I think, that I do.

Take the most intimate part of my heart.
Cure this wound that hurts me so.
Take away the thorn of this anguish.

Remove this fear from me,
this resentment, these temptations.

Jesus, what do you want from me?
How would you look at this person?
What would be your attitude
in this particular difficulty?
How would you behave in this situation?
May those who see me see you, Jesus.
Transform me into you completely.
May I become a living transparency
of your person.

This exercise must last from forty-five to fifty
minutes.

9. *Adoration in Encounter* (Elevation)

In this exercise one pronounces mentally or
in low voice, an expression which I will indicate
later.

Motivated by the phrase, the "I" goes out
towards the YOU. When you take on and live
the meaning of the expression, it captures your
attention, carries it, and deposits it on the YOU.

There is a movement or a going forth out of yourself. In this manner, the whole "I" remains in the whole YOU.

Stay calm, motionless. There is also a stillness.

Here is what I mean: there must not be any mental movement. You must not be preoccupied with the *meaning* of the phrase. In all understanding, there is a coming and going. As for ourselves, we are now in adoration. Therefore, there must not be any analytical activity.

On the contrary: the mind, prompted by the phrase, goes forth towards a YOU, silent and clinging admiringly, contemplatively, possessively, lovingly. For example, if you say, "You are the immutable eternity," you must not preoccupy yourself with understanding or analyzing how and why God is eternal, but look at him and calmly admire him.

After silencing your whole being, become aware in faith of the presence of the One in whom we exist, move, and are.

Begin to utter the sentence in a low voice. Try to live what the sentence says, until your soul becomes saturated with the substance of the phrase.

After you have said it, remain in silence about thirty seconds or more, quiet, as still as one who listens to an echo. The attention is motionless, possessively absorbed, identified with the substance of the phrase; that is, with God himself.

In this exercise, you must let yourself be seized by the YOU. The "I" practically disappears while the YOU controls the whole sphere.

Here are some expressions that may be used in this exercise:

You are my God.
For ever and ever you are God.
Your are motionless eternity.
You are infinite immensity.
You are without beginning or end.
You are so far and so close.
You are my all.
Oh, depth of the essence
and presence of my God!

You are my total rest.
Only in you do I feel peace.
You are strength.
You are my security.
You are my patience.
You are my joy.
You are my eternal life,
great and marvelous Lord.

10. "In Jesus' Place"

Imagine Jesus in adoration, at night, under the stars, or in the early morning.

With infinite reverence, in faith and peace, penetrate the heart of Jesus. Try to observe and revive what Jesus experience in his relationship with the Father, and you will thus participate in the profound experience of the Lord.

Try to scrutinize and live the feelings of admiration Jesus had toward the Father. Say, with the heart of Jesus, with his vibrations, for example, "glorify your name," "hallowed be your name."

Place yourself in the heart of Jesus, take on his harmony and generate the attitude of self-surrender and submission he experienced in the face of the Father's will when he said: "Let your will be done, not mine." "Your will be done."

Try to experience what he felt when he said, "for You and I are one," when he uttered, "Abba"—dear Father! Place yourself in the heart of Jesus to say the priestly prayer, chapter 17 in the Gospel according to Saint John.

In faith, make these—and so many more things—"yours" in the Spirit, in order to be clad with the inner disposition of Jesus. And return to everyday life carrying the profound life of Jesus.

This prayer will only be possible in the Holy Spirit, "who teaches the whole truth".

11. Contemplation

According to Saint John of the Cross, the signs that a soul has entered contemplation are the following:

- The soul likes to be alone with God in loving and quiet attention.

- Even if one seems to be wasting time, the soul is quiet and calm, attentive to God, in an inner peace and at rest.

- The soul is free from preoccupation, without thinking or meditating; only a sustained and loving concentration on God.

a) *Silence*. Empty yourself. Suspend all the activities or the senses. Silence your memories. Let go of your preoccupations.

Isolate yourself from both the outer and the inner world. Do not think about anything. Better still, do not think anything.

Stay beyond feeling and action. Do not concentrate on anything. Do not look at anything, either internally or externally.

Outside of me, nothing; inside of me; nothing.

What is left? An attention of myself to myserself, in silence and in peace.

b) *Presence*. Open one's attention to the Other, in faith, as when one looks without thinking, as one who loves and feels loved.

Avoid imagining God. All images or forms of God must disappear. It is better to "silence" any notion of the location of God. The verb that corresponds to God is the verb *to be*.

He *is* the pure, loving enveloping, penetrating, and omnipotent presence.

There only remains a You towards which I am an open, loving, and peaceful attention.

Practice the auditive exercise until the word "falls" by itself. Remain without uttering anything with your lips, anything with your mind.

To look and feel that your are being seen.
To love and feel loved.
I am like a beach. He is like the sea.
I am like a meadow. He is like the sun.
Let yourself be enlightened,
inundated, LOVED.
LET YOURSELF BE LOVED.

Formula for the exercise:

You search me.
You know me.
You love me.

12. Praying with Nature

If you are outdoors, facing a splendid land-scape, one of the methods of prayer you can use is praying with nature.

Start with the prayerful reading of Psalm 104. In the spirit of this Psalm, begin to contemplate, look and admire all that your eyes can see.

Continue to admire, impressed by each and everyone of the creatures in the Psalm: clouds, winds, snow-covered peaks, cascades, rivers, valleys, springs, birds, nests, streams, vales, plants, butterflies, flowers, grain, olive, vine-yards, age-old trees, minute grass blades, sun, moon, light, shadow.

For each creature you contemplate and ad-mire, say, "My God, how great you are" (v. 1).

Once in a while, repeat verse 24: "How countless are your works, Lord, all of them made so wisely! The earth is full of your creatures."

Listen, absorb and submerge yourself in the harmony of creation. Keep yourself concentrated and attentive to each one of the voices of the world: the thousands of insects that sing out their joy of living; the varied sound of so many birds; the murmur of the wind or of the river; crickets; frogs, roosters, dogs; all the living beings that express their joy of living and, in their own way, acclaim and gratefully sing to their Lord. In their name and with them, say, "All creatures of the Lord, bless the Lord."

Arouse in yourself a sensation of universal brotherhood: feel, in God, that each creature is your brother, your sister; feel that in God you are one with all that your eyes can see; submerge yourself in the great family of creation, without being conscious of it; feel yourself a joyous part of the happiness of living; that each of them experiences as if you swam in the sea of universal life and vibrated with the tenderness of the world.

Implore their forgiveness for being enslaved by man; for being trampled so often and for being treated with cruelty. Feel and express gratitude for all the benefits that creatures contribute to the bliss of man.

Enter into a close dialogue with one particular creature: a flower, a tree, a stone, water from a stream. Question it about its origin, its history, its health, and listen to it attentively. In an intimate dialogue, tell your own history to it. Admire it and thank it for its beauty, its perfume, its contribution to world harmony. Enter into a friendly communion with this creature.

During this long *prayer with nature*, always keep the Bible open in your hands; frequently insert verses 1, 24, 31, and 33 of Psalm 104 and also Psalm 8, especially the first refrain: "Lord, our God, how majestic is your name throughout the world."

13. Community Prayer

Community prayer, also called *shared*, occurs when a group gets together to pray, and it does so in the following manner: a) spontaneously; b) aloud; c) before each other; d) alternating individually—not everyone at the same time.

In order for community—or shared—prayer to be truly effective and convincing, the following conditions are necessary:

1. One assumes that the people who share prayer have previously deepened a personal relationship with the Lord. Otherwise, community prayer becomes an artificial and empty activity.

2. Each person must avoid, as much as possible, the repetition of short sentences, stereotypes, or formal and memorized expressions. On the contrary, one must pray spontaneously, from the heart, as if at this particular moment you were alone in the world with God. Pray informally and naturally.

3. To do this, those who pray must be convinced and remember that they carry great inner riches, more precious than they can imagine; that the Holy Spirit lives within them, and that he expresses himself through their mouth; this is why they must speak with ease and freedom.

4. It is to be expected that no emotional short-circuit may exist among those who pray. If between two persons or any others in the group there is a strong disagreement that is well-known and public, this conflict hinders the spontaneity of the group. The walls that separate one brother from another also separate these brothers from God.

5. It is also indispensable that sincerity and truth exist; that is to say, that the one who prays when expressing himself verbally, may not be motivated by pride to utter original or brilliant things. He must at all times rectify his intention, and express himself as if he were alone before God.

6. But the essential condition is that prayer be truly *shared*: when a member of the group speaks with the Lord, I must not only be one who hears or observes but—it is implied—that I also take on the words that come out of my brother's mouth, and with these same words I address myself to God. And when I vocalize my prayer, it is implied that my brothers take my words, and with these same words address themselves to

God. In this manner, *each one* prays *with each other* all the time. This is the secret behind the grandeur and richness of community prayer: the Holy Spirit overflows amidst such diverse personalities and histories; this is why the result is such an enriching prayer.

14. *Community Meditation*

Community or *shared meditation* occurs when various people get together to contemplate the Word of God or another theme, and to spontaneously express before the others what this theme or word suggests to them.

In order for community meditation to be truly effective and convincing, the conditions detailed for community prayer must be taken into consideration, especially numbers 3, 4, and 5.

Moreover, in order to acclimate oneself, it is advisable to begin with an invocation to the Holy Spirit and a brief, spontaneous prayer or a psalm.

It is also advisable to begin the meditation by reading a section of the Bible or any other book, in order to circumscribe the subject of meditation and shed light on the theme.

It is convenient to refer and make applications to life throughout the reflection, setting practical standards so that these criteria may become concrete decisions for fraternal life or pastoral activity.

15. Variants

a) Community Prayer Based on Psalms

In this prayer, each person has in front of him or her a given Psalm. The group first reads it together slowly; next, each one prays it in privacy and silence, following the method of *Prayerful Reading*.

After two minutes, anyone may pray out loud —always holding the psalm open in his hands, paraphrasing or commenting the verse that most attracted his/her attention. Afterward, another does the same. And so on, for all who wish to take part. End with a song.

b) Community Meditation Based on the Word

This is somewhat similar to the preceding variant. Each one holds the Bible open to a particular chapter, and one member of the group reads an excerpt. All remain silent while each person meditates in private, always holding the Bible open.

After this, anyone from the group comments —in the form of a reflection—on the verse that most struck him or her. Next, another does the same, and successively all who wish. End with a song.

16. Meditation

This spiritual activity is recommended for people who have an analytical mind. For them it is not sufficient just to meditate on a reading: they can and should advance deeper.

We must not forget that the great figures of God are formed in meditation.

Meditation is a mental activity, concentrated and precise, in which we choose a text or a theme and contemplate it as a whole and in its details. We analyze it in its causes and effects in relation to life criteria and value judgements; in other words, a mentality according to God's mind. In this way, criteria become convictions and convictions become decisions. In this manner, we are converted into *disciples of the Lord.*

To prepare

– Pray for light.

– Choose the material that will be meditated upon.

– In order to help the mind to concentrate, it is advisable to imagine the scene graphically: what are they talking about, how do they move, what is the setting, and other details.

To unravel and put in order

– Distinguish the different levels of a scene; look for the meaning and purpose of each word and for its context; the meaning of each scene and its context; linger on the significance of the verbs.

- Infer, deduce, explain, implement, combine different ideas, compare them.

- Look for the internal logic of cause and effect, principles and conclusions, what each thing is and what it is not. Distinguish reasons and intentions, actions and reactions, efforts and results.

To apply or to get involved

- I must *place myself* in the scene, as if I were an actor and not an observer: they speak to me and they question me—the words of Christ to Zacchaeus, to Peter, to the rich young man, to the blind man on the road, are addressed to me—and I, in turn, talk and question these persons in the scene.

- I compare what I hear in the scene with my problems, with my present situation, the events of our time.

- I end with a prayer.

IV. PROBLEMS OF FORGIVENESS

We are very seldom offended; very often we feel offended.

To forgive is to abandon or to eliminate an adverse feeling against our brother.

Who suffers? The one who hates or the one who is hated? The person hated generally lives happily in his world. The one who cultivates resentment is like the one who seizes a live coal or stirs up a flame. It would seem that the flame would burn his enemy; but no, it burns him. Resentment destroys only the resentful.

Pride is blind and suicidal: it prefers the satisfaction of vengeance to the relief of forgiveness. But to hate is absurd: it is like stocking up venom in one's guts. The resentful person lives in perpetual agony.

The most delicious fruit in the whole world is the sensation of rest and relief that is felt when forgiving, and there is no fatigue as unpleasant as the one produced by resentment. It is truly worthwhile to forgive, even if only out of personal interest, since no other therapy is more liberating than forgiveness.

It is not necessary to ask for forgiveness or to forgive only with words. Very often a greeting, a kind look, a conversation, or getting closer is sufficient. These are the best signs of forgiveness.

Sometimes it can occur that people forgive and feel the forgiveness; but after a while, aversion returns. Do not be surprised. A deep wound needs many healings. Forgive again and again until the wound is completely healed.

EXERCISES IN FORGIVING

In the Spirit of Jesus

1. In faith, place yourself in the spirit of Jesus. Assume his feelings. Face the "enemy" mentally: look at him through Jesus' eyes. Perceive him with Jesus' feelings, embrace him with Jesus' arms as if "you were" Jesus.

Concentrated, in full intimacy with the Lord Jesus and with the "enemy" placed in the back of your memory say to the Lord: Jesus, come within me. Take possession of my being. Calm my hostilities. Give me your heart, poor and humble. I wish to feel towards this enemy what you felt towards him when you died for him. With your feelings intimately united to mine, I forgive; with you, I love, I embrace this person, He or She-You-I, one being. I-You-He-or She, one unity.

Repeat these or similar words for about thirty minutes.

Forgiveness through Understanding

2. If we could understand, we would not have to forgive. Bring the "enemy" back to your memory and apply the following thoughts to him.

Except in very rare cases, no one acts with bad intentions. Are you not ascribing to this person wicked intentions he never had? In the end, who is mistaken? If he makes you suffer, have you thought how much you make him suffer? Who knows if he really said what they told you he had said? Who knows if he said it with a different tone of voice, or in a different context?

He seems proud; it is not pride, it is shyness. He seems stubborn; it is not obstinacy; it is a reflex of self-affirmation. His conduct seems aggressive towards you; it is not aggressiveness, it is self-defense, a way to protect himself. He does not attack you, he defends himself. And you assume his heart is full of wickedness. Who is unjust and wrong?

Of course, you find him troublesome; he may be more so to himself. It is true you suffer because of his ways; but he suffers much more himself. If there is one person on earth who is interested in not being this way, it is not you, it is he. He would like to please everyone; he cannot. He would like to live in peace with all; he cannot. He would like to be charming; he cannot. If he had chosen his ways, he would be the most gracious person in the world. Does it makes sense for you to be irritated by a way of being he has not chosen? Is he as guilty as you suppose him to be? In the end, is it not you, with your assumptions and repulsions, who are more unjust than he is?

If we understood, there would be no need to forgive.

Letting go

3. This is an act of the mind by which we release our attention to the person who has become an enemy. You interrupt this link of attention—by which your mind was tied to this person—and remain disconnected from him and in peace.

You are not to violently expel this person from your mind, because he would become more affixed. What happens here is that you suspend for a moment that mental activity, you make a mental vacuum, and the "enemy" disappears. He will come back. Once more, suspend your mental activity or turn your attention towards something else.

There are a few popular verbs that signify this forgiveness: *To untie:* the attention is tied down, untie it. *To unfasten:* it is fastened, unfasten it.

To let go: the memory grasps, let it go. *To abandon. To forget.*

As you see, this is not forgiveness as such, but it does have its effects. It might be the first step, especially for a moral injury recently suffered.

V. HOW TO LIVE
A DESERT

The only way to revitalize the things of God is by revitalizing the heart. When the heart is filled with God, the things of life are filled with the enchantment of God. And the heart is brought back to life during "Intense Moments". Thus did the prophets, the saints, and above all, Christ.

An "Intense Moment" is time set aside to be with the Lord, segments of time during the daily activities, for example, thirty minutes a day, a few hours every two weeks, etc. "Intense Moments" are intended not only for praying but also for the recuperation of emotional balance, interior unity, serenity, and peace. Otherwise, people disintegrate in the insanity of life.

Those who wish to take seriously their life with God need to include the system of "Intense Moments" in their schedule of activities. If you keep your "Intense Moments", "Intense Moments" will save you from the emptiness of life and existential vacuum. If you complain that you have no time, I will tell you that time is a question of preference and preferences depend on priorities. We have time for what we prefer.

When one whole day is dedicated to the Lord—at least seven hours—in silence and solitude, this day is called a *desert*.

In order to live a *desert* it is advisable, and almost necessary to leave the place where one lives or work, and to withdraw to a solitary location in the country, in a forest, on a mountain, or in a retreat house.

It is wise to live the *desert* in small groups, of three to five for example. But, once you have reached the location where you will spend the day, it is essential to separate, so that each person can remain absolutely alone. In the final hours, you may come together to fraternally exchange experiences and to pray as a community.

It is desirable that each person take along something to eat, while remembering the *desert* also has a penitential nature. Nonetheless in order to avoid dehydration you must not abstain from taking liquids.

In short. A *desert* is a time of retreat dedicated to God in silence, solitude, and penance.

It is recommendable to have with you an assortment of biblical texts, psalms, and exercises for relaxation—these are all found in this book. Do not forget to take a notebook along to jot down your impressions.

Guidelines

1. Use these guidelines with flexibility, since the Holy Spirit may have others plans. You must give leeway to the spontaneity of grace. For example, feel free with regards to time schedule for each point.

2. Once you have reached the location where you will spend the day, begin with a prayerful reading of the psalms. This is necessary to prepare a favorable atmosphere for a deeper spiritual level. About sixty minutes.

3. If your thoughts feel scattered, prepare yourself with exercises for relaxation, concentration, and silence. About thirty minutes. You may repeat these exercises throughout the day; but from the very beginning, you must achieve an elementary state of serenity.

4. Personal dialogue with the Lord God is not necessarily a dialogue of words, but of inner dialogue. To talk to God, to be with Him, to love and to feel loved. This is the most important spiritual attitude of the *desert*. You may use the techniques described above. Around seventy-five minutes.

5. Since this is a day of intense cerebral activity, it is good to have a few brief intervals of rest when the most important thing is to do nothing but rest.

6. A *desert* cannot exist without a prolonged *meditated reading* following the method explained in the second technique. Use biblical texts. Compare your personal and apostolic life with the word of God. About eighty minutes.

7. There must also be a pleasant and lengthy dialogue with Jesus Christ, explicitly with him. Talk with him as a friend speaks to a friend, walk with him in your imagination solving difficulties on the road of life. About fifty minutes.

8. Do an intense exercise of self-surrender: to heal the wounds again, to accept so many things that have been rejected, to forgive oneself and to forgive others, to strengthen peace. About forty minutes.

Have the practical guidelines of this book close at hand. Do not become euphoric when consolation arises, nor depressed when aridity creeps in. The criteria of the divine presence is peace. If you have peace, even in deep aridity, God is with you. Remember how many deserts Jesus lived.

BIBLE REFERENCES FOR THE DESERT

To go to the desert is to go on a pilgrimage, like the People of God who searched for the face of God.

Old Testament

Moses encounters God in the desert: Ex 3: 1-15.

God leads the People of Israel through the desert: Ex 14-20; 24; Nb 9:15-24.

The face of God leads Moses through the desert: Ex 33:7-23.

The steps of the desert: Nb 10-14; 16; 17; 20.

The desert, a place where God is manifest: Ex 19.

Elijah encounters God in the desert: 1K 19: 3-15.

The desert, a place of purification: Nb 20: 1-13.

New Testament

John, greatest of prophets, in the desert: Lk 1:13-17; 3:1-6; Mk 1:1-8; Mt 3:1-13.

Jesus, man of the desert.

Thirty years of silence and anonymity: Lk 3:23.

Immediate preparation for his mission leads to the desert: Lk 4:1-13; Mt 4:1-11; Mk 1:12.

Jesus withdraws in total solitude to be with the Father: Lk 6:12; Mt 14:13; Mk 6:46; Mt 14:23; Jn 6:15; Mk 7:24; Lk 9:10; Mk 1:35; Mt 6:6; Mk 14:32; Mt 17:1; Lk 9:28; Mt 26:26; Lk 22:39; Mk 9:2; Lk 3:21; Lk 4:1-13; Lk 9:18; Lk 21:37; Lk 4:42; Lk 5:1; Lk 11:1.

Paul spends three years in the desert: Ga 1:15-18.

John remains alone in his exile in Asia Minor: Rv 1:9f.

BIBLE TEXTS FOR INTENSE MOMENTS

Psalms: 16, 23, 25, 27, 31, 36, 40, 42, 51, 56, 61, 62, 63, 69, 71, 77, 84, 86, 88, 90, 91, 93, 96, 103, 104, 118, 119, 123, 126, 130, 131, 139, 143.

(Please be aware that I use the numbering of the Hebrew Bible which is adopted by all our modern editions. Books of Divine Office follow the numbering of the *Vulgate*, for which we have to subtract one.)

Magnificence of God: Is 2:9-23; 40:12-31; 41: 21-29; 44:1-9.

Prophetic Call: Jr 1:4-11; Is 49:1-7.

Apostolic Life: 1 Co 4:9-14; 2 Co 4:1-18; 2 Co 6:3-11; 2 Co 11:23-30.

Patience: Eccl. 2:1-7.

Compassion of God: Ho 2:16-25; Is 41:8-20; Os 11:1-6.

Irresistible faith: Rm 8:28-39.

Divine filiation: Rm 8:15-22.

Courage and Hope: Jos 1; Is 43; Is 54; Is 60.

Christ, Center of the World: Col 1:15-21; Ep 3:14-21.

Historical Texts: Ac 14-28; 2Tm; 1 M chapters 2 to 5; 2 M chapters 5 to 8.

Jesus merciful and compassionate: Mt 9:35; Mk 1:41; Mt 14:14; Lk 7:13; Mk 2:17; Mt 11:19; Mt 9:9; Lk 15:1f; Mt 9:13; Lk 7:36, Jn 8:1f.

Jesus, meek, patient, and humble: Mk 3:10; Lk 5:1; Mt 5:5; Mk 14:56; Mt 27:13, Lk 23:8; Lk 23:24; Mt 4:1-11; 2 Co 10:1; 1 P 2:23.

The option of Jesus for the poor: Mt 9:36; Mk 6:34; Lk 6:20; Mt 11:5; Lk 4:18; Mt 25:34f.

Jesus sincere and true: Mt 5:37; Mt 16:21;

Lk 13:32; Jn 8:40f; Jn 6:66; Mt 7:3; Lk 7:39; Jn 8:32; Jn 18:37; 1 P 2:22.

To love as Jesus loved: Jn 13:34; Mt 19:14; Jn 11:1f; Jn 15:15; Jn 20:27; Mk 10:45; Mt 20:28; Jn 15:9; Jn 3:16; Ga 2:20.

Printed in Canada

 **Transcontinental
Printing Inc.**
MÉTROLITHO DIVISION